TYGER TYGER, BURNING BRIGHT

By the same author:

Best-Loved Poems: A Treasury of Verse (ed.)

I Wandered Lonely As a Cloud: . . . and other poems you half-remember from school (ed.)

Poems to Learn by Heart (ed.)

TYGER TYGER, BURNING BRIGHT

Much-Loved Poems You Half-Remember

Ana Sampson

Michael O'Mara Books Limited

This new edition published in 2023
First published in Great Britain in 2011 by
Michael O'Mara Books Limited
9 Lion Yard
Tremadoc Road
London SW4 7NQ

A CIP catalogue record for this book is available from the British Library.

This product is made of material from well-managed, FSC®-certified forests
and other controlled sources. The manufacturing processes conform to the
environmental regulations of the country of origin.

ISBN: 978-1-78929-546-7

1 2 3 4 5 6 7 8 9 10

www.mombooks.com

Cover illustration by Sarah Dennis
Cover design by Natasha Le Coultre

Printed and bound by CPI Group (UK) Ltd, Croydon, CR0 4YY

CONTENTS

For my mother, who taught me that you can never be reading too many books at once.

INTRODUCTION

Some years ago I embarked upon the task of putting together a collection of all those poems you half-remembered from school. The aim was to compile an anthology of all the verses that contained those vaguely, and sometimes mistakenly, recalled lines that have somehow stubbornly stuck in our memories from childhood and beyond, and prove along the way that we all know far more poetry than we think we do. It wasn't enough. Every reader, and every colleague and friend, found some almost unforgivable omission in the first volume, *I Wandered Lonely as a Cloud…: and other poems you half-remember from school*, and, unfortunately, none of them were shy about telling me so! This volume has therefore been an attempt to include many of the much-loved poems that people told me they missed in that book, as well as revisiting some lesser known verses that I hoped readers would find as enjoyable as I had while putting this collection together.

This anthology is arranged according to theme, which is never an easy task. A poet may be talking about love at the same time as death, or nature at the same time as whatever he or she understands by God, so the categories are often fluid. Some poems that defied categorization – but were just too wonderful to omit – have been gathered at the end, in a section that I hope you will agree contains some delightful and unusual works. Each chapter aims to bring a breadth of voices, eras and styles together to show how poets, at every time in history, have addressed the same eternal subjects, bringing to them their own experiences, prejudices, voices and rhythms. We change a great deal through the ages in our language and references, but in revisiting these poems I had to conclude that our preoccupations, our values and what perplexes us have changed amazingly little through time.

*

I love to be given a little background while reading a poem. I want to know: did the poet wrestle with his beautifully hymned faith? What was the outcome of the relationship – or was it perhaps an unrequited infatuation? – so passionately described here? If this verse was written in the trenches of a grisly and inhuman war, did the poet survive those dark days? Did this writer, so apparently passionate in the cause of rebellion and anarchy when he penned these words, live out his latter days as a contented pillar of the Establishment? I have tried to answer these questions by including some notes and incidental detail on the poets and poems: not enough to compose an authoritative biography, but some incidents and anecdotes which – I hope – shed a little light on the wonderful words themselves. I do hope that you have as much fun dipping into the collection as I had compiling it and researching the men and women who have left us such well-loved and familiar works.

ANA SAMPSON

ONE

'Green to the very door' – The Natural World

Beasts – from Blake's fearsome Tyger to the roly-poly yet graceful Jellicle cat – have always inspired poets and birds, especially, seem to stir writers to imaginative flight. In earlier times poets hymned nature's mysteries and, more recently, lamented the tide of progress that began to sweep away the countryside. Wordsworth's verses about nature's sublime beauty were already nostalgic for the pre-Industrial landscape by the time they were published, and poets including Gerald Manley Hopkins follow in his footsteps as the advocates of nature against the depredations of the modern world. I have included poems in this section that I hope will have the effect of a good lungful of country air on even the most metropolitan of readers.

Alexander Pope (1688–1744)

Ode on Solitude

Happy the man, whose wish and care
A few paternal acres bound,
Content to breathe his native air,
In his own ground.

Whose herds with milk, whose fields with bread,
Whose flocks supply him with attire,
Whose trees in summer yield him shade,
In winter fire.

Blest! who can unconcern'dly find
Hours, days, and years slide soft away,
In health of body, peace of mind,
Quiet by day,

Sound sleep by night; study and ease
Together mix'd; sweet recreation,
And innocence, which most does please,
With meditation.

Thus let me live, unseen, unknown;
Thus unlamented let me die;
Steal from the world, and not a stone
Tell where I lie.

Ted Hughes (1930–98)

Hawk Roosting

I sit in the top of the wood, my eyes closed.
Inaction, no falsifying dream
Between my hooked head and hooked feet:
Or in sleep rehearse perfect kills and eat.

The convenience of the high trees!
The air's buoyancy and the sun's ray
Are of advantage to me;
And the earth's face upward for my inspection.

My feet are locked upon the rough bark.
It took the whole of Creation
To produce my foot, my each feather:
Now I hold Creation in my foot

Or fly up, and revolve it all slowly –
I kill where I please because it is all mine.
There is no sophistry in my body:
My manners are tearing off heads –

The allotment of death.
For the one path of my flight is direct
Through the bones of the living.
No arguments assert my right:

The sun is behind me.
Nothing has changed since I began.
My eye has permitted no change.
I am going to keep things like this.

Gerard Manley Hopkins (1844–89)

Binsey Poplars

My aspens dear, whose airy cages quelled,
Quelled or quenched in leaves the leaping sun,
All felled, felled, are all felled;
Of a fresh and following folded rank
Not spared, not one
That dandled a sandalled
Shadow that swam or sank
On meadow and river and wind-wandering weed-winding bank.

O if we but knew what we do
When we delve or hew –
Hack and rack the growing green!
Since country is so tender
To touch, her being so slender,
That, like this sleek and seeing ball
But a prick will make no eye at all,
Where we, even where we mean
To mend her we end her,
When we hew or delve:
After-comers cannot guess the beauty been.
Ten or twelve, only ten or twelve
Strokes of havoc unselve
The sweet especial scene,
Rural scene, a rural scene,
Sweet especial rural scene.

The Windhover

To Christ our Lord

I caught this morning morning's minion, king-
      dom of daylight's dauphin, dapple-dawn-drawn Falcon, in
        his riding
      Of the rolling level underneath him steady air, and striding
High there, how he rung upon the rein of a wimpling wing

In his ecstasy! then off, off forth on swing,
      As a skate's heel sweeps smooth on a bow-bend: the hurl
        and gliding
      Rebuffed the big wind. My heart in hiding

Stirred for a bird, – the achieve of, the mastery of the thing!
      Brute beauty and valour and act, oh, air, pride, plume,
        here
      Buckle! AND the fire that breaks from thee then, a billion
Times told lovelier, more dangerous, O my chevalier!

      No wonder of it: shéer plód makes plough down sillion
Shine, and blue-bleak embers, ah my dear,
      Fall, gall themselves, and gash gold-vermilion.

Rudyard Kipling (1865–1936)

The Way Through The Woods

They shut the road through the woods
Seventy years ago.
Weather and rain have undone it again,
And now you would never know
There was once a road through the woods
Before they planted the trees.
It is underneath the coppice and heath,
And the thin anemones.
Only the keeper sees
That, where the ring-dove broods,
And the badgers roll at ease,
There was once a road through the woods.

Yet, if you enter the woods
Of a summer evening late,
When the night-air cools on the trout-ringed pools
Where the otter whistles his mate,
(They fear not men in the woods,
Because they see so few.)
You will hear the beat of a horse's feet,
And the swish of a skirt in the dew,
Steadily cantering through
The misty solitudes,
As though they perfectly knew
The old lost road through the woods.
But there is no road through the woods...

The Glory of the Garden

Our England is a garden that is full of stately views,
Of borders, beds and shrubberies and lawns and avenues,
With statues on the terraces and peacocks strutting by;
But the Glory of the Garden lies in more than meets the eye.

For where the thick laurels grow, along the thin red wall,
You will find the tool- and potting-sheds which are the
      heart of all;
The cold-frames and the hot-houses, the dungpits and the tanks,
The rollers, carts and drain-pipes, with the barrows and
      the planks.

And there you'll see the gardeners, the men and 'prentice boys
Told off to do as they are bid and do it without noise;
For, except when seeds are planted and we shout to scare
      the birds,
The Glory of the Garden it abideth not in words.

And some can pot begonias and some can bud a rose,
And some are hardly fit to trust with anything that grows;
But they can roll and trim the lawns and sift the sand and loam,
For the Glory of the Garden occupieth all who come.

Our England is a garden, and such gardens are not made
By singing:– 'Oh, how beautiful!' and sitting in the shade,
While better men than we go out and start their working lives
At grubbing weeds from gravel-paths with broken dinner-knives.

There's not a pair of legs so thin, there's not a head so thick,
There's not a hand so weak and white, nor yet a heart so sick,
But it can find some needful job that's crying to be done,
For the Glory of the Garden glorifieth every one.

Then seek your job with thankfulness and work till
    further orders,
If it's only netting strawberries or killing slugs on borders;
And when your back stops aching and your hands begin
    to harden,
You will find yourself a partner in the Glory of the Garden.

Oh, Adam was a gardener, and God who made him sees
That half a proper gardener's work is done upon his knees,
So when your work is finished, you can wash your hands
    and pray
For the Glory of the Garden, that it may not pass away!

And the Glory of the Garden it shall never pass away!

Anonymous (mid-thirteenth century)

Sumer is icumen in

Sumer is icumen in –
Lhude sing, cuccu!
Groweth sed and bloweth med
And springth the wude nu,
Sing cuccu!

Awe bleteth after lomb,
Lhouth after calve cu.
Bulluc sterteth, bucke verteth.
Murie sing, cuccu!
Cuccu, cuccu,
Wel singes thu, cuccu!
Ne swik thu naver nu!

Sing, cuccu, nu! Sing, cuccu!
Sing, cuccu! Sing, cuccu, nu!

(*Lhude* – loud; *sed* – seed; *med* – mead; *wude* – wood; *nu* – anew;
awe – ewe; *lomb* – lamb; *llouth* – lows; *cu* – cow; *sterteth* – starts;
verteth – farts; *murie* – merrily; *thu* – thou; *swik* – stop; *naver* –
never; *nu* – now.)

Abraham Cowley (1618–67)

Drinking

The thirsty earth soaks up the rain,
And drinks and gapes for drink again;
The plants suck in the earth, and are
With constant drinking fresh and fair;
The sea itself (which one would think
Should have but little need of drink)
Drinks ten thousand rivers up,
So fill'd that they o'erflow the cup.
The busy Sun (and one would guess
By's drunken fiery face no less)
Drinks up the sea, and when h'as done,
The Moon and Stars drink up the Sun:
    They drink and dance by their own light,
They drink and revel all the night:
Nothing in Nature's sober found,
But an eternal health goes round.
Fill up the bowl, then, fill it high,
Fill all the glasses there – for why
Should every creature drink but I?
Why, man of morals, tell me why?

William Blake (1757–1827)

The Tyger

Tyger Tyger, burning bright,
In the forests of the night:
What immortal hand or eye,
Could frame thy fearful symmetry?

In what distant deeps or skies
Burnt the fire of thine eyes?
On what wings dare he aspire?
What the hand, dare seize the fire?

And what shoulder, and what art,
Could twist the sinews of thy heart?
And when thy heart began to beat,
What dread hand? and what dread feet?

What the hammer? what the chain?
In what furnace was thy brain?
What the anvil? what dread grasp,
Dare its deadly terrors clasp?

When the stars threw down their spears
And water'd heaven with their tears:
Did he smile his work to see?
Did he who made the Lamb make thee?

Tyger, Tyger burning bright,
In the forests of the night:
What immortal hand or eye,
Dare frame thy fearful symmetry?

Auguries of Innocence [extract]

To see a world in a grain of sand,
And a heaven in a wild flower
Hold infinity in the palm of your hand,
And eternity in an hour

A robin redbreast in a cage
Puts all heaven in a rage.

A dove-house fill'd with doves and pigeons
Shudders hell thro' all its regions.
A dog starv'd at his master's gate
Predicts the ruin of the state.

A horse misused upon the road
Calls to heaven for human blood.
Each outcry of the hunted hare
A fibre from the brain does tear.

A skylark wounded in the wing,
A cherubim does cease to sing.
The game-cock clipt and arm'd for fight
Does the rising sun affright.

Every wolf's and lion's howl
Raises from hell a human soul.

W. H. Davies (1871–1940)

The Kingfisher

It was the Rainbow gave thee birth,
And left thee all her lovely hues;
And, as her mother's name was Tears,
So runs it in my blood to choose
For haunts the lonely pools, and keep
In company with trees that weep.
Go you and, with such glorious hues,
Live with proud peacocks in green parks;
On lawns as smooth as shining glass,
Let every feather show its marks;
Get thee on boughs and clap thy wings
Before the windows of proud kings.
Nay, lovely Bird, thou art not vain;
Thou hast no proud, ambitious mind;
I also love a quiet place
That's green, away from all mankind;
A lonely pool, and let a tree
Sigh with her bosom over me.

William Wordsworth (1770–1850)

Lines Composed a Few Miles above Tintern Abbey, on Revisiting the Banks of the Wye during a tour. July 13, 1798 [extract]

Five years have past; five summers, with the length
Of five long winters! and again I hear
These waters, rolling from their mountain-springs
With a soft inland murmur. Once again
Do I behold these steep and lofty cliffs,
That on a wild secluded scene impress
Thoughts of more deep seclusion; and connect
The landscape with the quiet of the sky.
The day is come when I again repose
Here, under this dark sycamore, and view
These plots of cottage-ground, these orchard-tufts,
Which at this season, with their unripe fruits,
Are clad in one green hue, and lose themselves
'Mid groves and copses. Once again I see
These hedge-rows, hardly hedge-rows, little lines
Of sportive wood run wild: these pastoral farms,
Green to the very door; and wreaths of smoke
Sent up, in silence, from among the trees!
With some uncertain notice, as might seem
Of vagrant dwellers in the houseless woods,
Or of some Hermit's cave, where by his fire
The Hermit sits alone.

T. S. Eliot (1888–1965)

Song of the Jellicles

Jellicle Cats come out tonight,
Jellicle Cats come one come all:
The Jellicle Moon is shining bright –
Jellicles come to the Jellicle Ball.

Jellicle Cats are black and white,
Jellicle Cats are rather small;
Jellicle Cats are merry and bright,
And pleasant to hear when they caterwaul.
Jellicle Cats have cheerful faces,
Jellicle Cats have bright black eyes;
They like to practise their airs and graces
And wait for the Jellicle Moon to rise.

Jellicle Cats develop slowly,
Jellicle Cats are not too big;
Jellicle Cats are roly-poly,
They know how to dance a gavotte and a jig.
Until the Jellicle Moon appears
They make their toilette and take their repose:
Jellicles wash behind their ears,
Jellicles dry between their toes.

Jellicle Cats are white and black,
Jellicle Cats are of moderate size;
Jellicles jump like a jumping-jack,
Jellicle Cats have moonlit eyes.
They're quiet enough in the morning hours,
They're quiet enough in the afternoon,
Reserving their terpsichorean powers
To dance by the light of the Jellicle Moon.

Jellicle Cats are black and white,
Jellicle Cats (as I said) are small;
If it happens to be a stormy night
They will practise a caper or two in the hall.
If it happens the sun is shining bright
You would say they had nothing to do at all:
They are resting and saving themselves to be right
For the Jellicle Moon and the Jellicle Ball.

Percy Bysshe Shelley (1792–1822)

Ode to the West Wind [extract]

I

O wild West Wind, thou breath of Autumn's being,
Thou, from whose unseen presence the leaves dead
Are driven, like ghosts from an enchanter fleeing,

Yellow, and black, and pale, and hectic red,
Pestilence-stricken multitudes: O thou,
Who chariotest to their dark wintry bed

The wingèd seeds, where they lie cold and low,
Each like a corpse within its grave, until
Thine azure sister of the spring shall blow

Her clarion o'er the dreaming earth, and fill
(Driving sweet buds like flocks to feed in air)
With living hues and odours plain and hill:

Wild Spirit, which art moving everywhere;
Destroyer and preserver; hear, oh, hear!

II.

Thou on whose stream, mid the steep sky's commotion,
Loose clouds like earth's decaying leaves are shed,
Shook from the tangled boughs of Heaven and Ocean,

Angels of rain and lightning: there are spread
On the blue surface of thine aëry surge,
Like the bright hair uplifted from the head

Of some fierce Mænad, even from the dim verge
Of the horizon to the zenith's height,
The locks of the approaching storm. Thou dirge

Of the dying year, to which this closing night
Will be the dome of a vast sepulchre,
Vaulted with all thy congregated might

Of vapours, from whose solid atmosphere
Black rain, and fire, and hail, will burst: oh hear!

Seamus Heaney (1939–2013)

Blackberry Picking

Late August, given heavy rain and sun
For a full week, the blackberries would ripen.
At first, just one, a glossy purple clot
Among others, red, green, hard as a knot.
You ate that first one and its flesh was sweet
Like thickened wine: summer's blood was in it
Leaving stains upon the tongue and lust for
Picking. Then red ones inked up and that hunger
Sent us out with milk cans, pea tins, jam-pots
Where briars scratched and wet grass bleached our boots.
Round hayfields, cornfields and potato-drills
We trekked and picked until the cans were full,
Until the tinkling bottom had been covered
With green ones, and on top big dark blobs burned
Like a plate of eyes. Our hands were peppered
With thorn pricks, our palms sticky as Bluebeard's.

We hoarded the fresh berries in the byre.
But when the bath was filled we found a fur,
A rat-grey fungus, glutting on our cache.
The juice was stinking too. Once off the bush
The fruit fermented, the sweet flesh would turn sour.
I always felt like crying. It wasn't fair
That all the lovely canfuls smelt of rot.
Each year I hoped they'd keep, knew they would not.

Robert Burns (1759–96)

To a Mouse, On Turning Her up in Her Nest With the Plough, November 1785

Wee, sleeket, cowran, tim'rous *beastie*,
O, what a panic's in thy breastie!
Thou need na start awa sae hasty,
      Wi' bickering brattle!
I wad be laith to rin an' chase thee,
      Wi' murd'ring *pattle*!

I'm truly sorry Man's dominion
Has broken Nature's social union,
An' justifies that ill opinion
      Which makes thee startle,
At me, thy poor, earth-born companion,
      An' *fellow-mortal*!

I doubt na, whyles, but thou may thieve;
What then? poor beastie, thou maun live!
A *daimen-icker* in a *thrave*
      'S a sma' request:
I'll get a blessin' wi' the lave,
      And never miss't!

Thy wee bit *housie*, too, in ruin!
It's silly wa's the win's are strewin!
And naething, now, to big a new ane,
      O' foggage green!
An' bleak December's winds ensuin,
      Baith snell an keen!

Thou saw the fields laid bare an' wast
An' weary Winter comin fast,

An' cozie here, beneath the blast,
    Thou thought to dwell,
Till, crash! the cruel *coulter* past
    Out thro' thy cell.

That wee bit heap o' leaves an' stibble
Has cost thee monie a weary nibble!
Now thou's turn'd out, for a' thy trouble,
    But house or hald,
To thole the Winter's sleety dribble
    An' *cranreuch* cauld!

But, Mousie, thou art no thy-lane,
In proving *foresight* may be vain:
The best laid schemes o' *Mice* an' *Men*,
    Gang aft agley,
An lea'e us nought but grief an' pain,
    For promis'd joy.

Still thou art blest, compared wi' *me*!
The *present* only toucheth thee:
But Och! I *backward* cast my e'e,
    On prospects drear!
An' *forward*, tho' I canna *see*,
    I *guess* an' *fear*!

(*brattle* – hurry; *laith* – loath; *pattle* – implement for cleaning
a plough; *daimen* – occasional; *icker* – ear of corn; *thrave* – two
stooks of cut corn; *lave* – the remainder; *wa's* – walls; *big* – build;
foggage – cow pasture; *snell* – biting; *coulter* – iron blade fixed
ahead of the ploughshare; *hald* – home; *cranreuch* – hoar-frost;
no thy-lane – not on your own; *agley* – askew, awry)

John Keats (1795–1821)

Ode to a Nightingale

My heart aches, and a drowsy numbness pains
My sense, as though of hemlock I had drunk,
Or emptied some dull opiate to the drains
One minute past, and Lethe-wards had sunk:
'Tis not through envy of thy happy lot,
But being too happy in thy happiness, –
That thou, light-wingèd Dryad of the trees,
In some melodious plot
Of beechen green, and shadows numberless,
Singest of summer in full-throated ease.

O for a draught of vintage! that hath been
Cooled a long age in the deep-delvèd earth,
Tasting of Flora and the country green,
Dance, and Provençal song, and sunburnt mirth!
O for a beaker full of the warm South,
Full of the true, the blushful Hippocrene,
With beaded bubbles winking at the brim,
And purple-stainèd mouth,
That I might drink, and leave the world unseen,
And with thee fade away into the forest dim –

Fade far away, dissolve, and quite forget
What thou among the leaves hast never known,
The weariness, the fever, and the fret
Here, where men sit and hear each other groan;
Where palsy shakes a few, sad, last grey hairs,
Where youth grows pale, and spectre-thin, and dies;
Where but to think is to be full of sorrow
And leaden-eyed despairs;

Where Beauty cannot keep her lustrous eyes,
Or new Love pine at them beyond to-morrow.

Away! away! for I will fly to thee,
Not charioted by Bacchus and his pards,
But on the viewless wings of Poesy,
Though the dull brain perplexes and retards:
Already with thee! tender is the night,
And haply the Queen-Moon is on her throne,
Clustered around by all her starry Fays;
But here there is no light,
Save what from heaven is with the breezes blown
Through verdurous glooms and winding mossy ways.

I cannot see what flowers are at my feet,
Nor what soft incense hangs upon the boughs,
But, in embalmèd darkness, guess each sweet
Wherewith the seasonable month endows
The grass, the thicket, and the fruit-tree wild –
White hawthorn, and the pastoral eglantine;
Fast-fading violets covered up in leaves;
And mid-May's eldest child,
The coming musk-rose, full of dewy wine,
The murmurous haunt of flies on summer eves.

Darkling I listen; and for many a time
I have been half in love with easeful Death,
Called him soft names in many a musèd rhyme,
To take into the air my quiet breath;
Now more than ever seems it rich to die,
To cease upon the midnight with no pain,
While thou art pouring forth thy soul abroad
In such an ecstasy!

Still wouldst thou sing, and I have ears in vain –
To thy high requiem become a sod.

Thou wast not born for death, immortal Bird!
No hungry generations tread thee down;
The voice I hear this passing night was heard
In ancient days by emperor and clown:
Perhaps the self-same song that found a path
Through the sad heart of Ruth, when, sick for home,
She stood in tears amid the alien corn;
The same that oft-times hath
Charmed magic casements, opening on the foam
Of perilous seas, in faery lands forlorn.

Forlorn! the very word is like a bell
To toll me back from thee to my sole self!
Adieu! the fancy cannot cheat so well
As she is famed to do, deceiving elf.
Adieu! adieu! thy plaintive anthem fades
Past the near meadows, over the still stream,
Up the hill-side; and now 'tis buried deep
In the next valley-glades:
Was it a vision, or a waking dream?
Fled is that music – Do I wake or sleep?

Endymion [extract]

BOOK I

A thing of beauty is a joy for ever:
Its loveliness increases; it will never
Pass into nothingness; but still will keep
A bower quiet for us, and a sleep
Full of sweet dreams, and health, and quiet breathing.

Therefore, on every morrow, are we wreathing
A flowery band to bind us to the earth,
Spite of despondence, of the inhuman dearth
Of noble natures, of the gloomy days,
Of all the unhealthy and o'er-darkened ways
Made for our searching: yes, in spite of all,
Some shape of beauty moves away the pall
From our dark spirits. Such the sun, the moon,
Trees old and young, sprouting a shady boon
For simple sheep; and such are daffodils
With the green world they live in; and clear rills
That for themselves a cooling covert make
'Gainst the hot season; the mid forest brake,
Rich with a sprinkling of fair musk-rose blooms:
And such too is the grandeur of the dooms
We have imagined for the mighty dead;
All lovely tales that we have heard or read–
An endless fountain of immortal drink,
Pouring unto us from the heaven's brink.

Thomas Hood (1799–1845)

No!

No sun – no moon!
No morn – no noon!
No dawn – no dusk – no proper time of day –
No sky – no earthly view –
No distance looking blue –
No road – no street – no 't'other side this way' –
No end to any Row –
No indications where the Crescents go –

No top to any steeple –
No recognitions of familiar people –
No courtesies for showing 'em –
No knowing 'em!
No travelling at all – no locomotion –
No inkling of the way – no notion –
'No go' by land or ocean –
No mail – no post –
No news from any foreign coast –
No Park, no Ring, no afternoon gentility –
No company – no nobility –
No warmth, no cheerfulness, no healthful ease,
No comfortable feel in any member –
No shade, no shine, no butterflies, no bees,
No fruits, no flowers, no leaves, no birds –
November!

Mary Howitt (1799–1888)

The Spider and the Fly

'Will you walk into my parlour?' said the Spider to the Fly,
''Tis the prettiest little parlour that ever you did spy;
The way into my parlour is up a winding stair,
And I've a many curious things to shew when you are there.'
'Oh no, no,' said the little Fly, 'to ask me is in vain,
For who goes up your winding stair can ne'er come down again.'

'I'm sure you must be weary, dear, with soaring up so high;
Will you rest upon my little bed?' said the Spider to the Fly.
'There are pretty curtains drawn around; the sheets are fine
    and thin,

And if you like to rest awhile, I'll snugly tuck you in!'
Oh no, no,' said the little Fly, 'for I've often heard it said,
They never, never wake again, who sleep upon your bed!'

Said the cunning Spider to the Fly, 'Dear friend what can I do,
To prove the warm affection I've always felt for you?
I have within my pantry, good store of all that's nice;
I'm sure you're very welcome – will you please to take a slice?'
'Oh no, no,' said the little Fly, 'kind Sir, that cannot be,
I've heard what's in your pantry, and I do not wish to see!'

'Sweet creature!' said the Spider, 'you're witty and you're wise,
How handsome are your gauzy wings, how brilliant are
        your eyes!
I've a little looking-glass upon my parlour shelf,
If you'll step in one moment, dear, you shall behold yourself.'
'I thank you, gentle Sir,' she said, 'for what you're pleased to say,
And bidding you good morning now, I'll call another day.'

The Spider turned him round about, and went into his den,
For well he knew the silly Fly would soon come back again:
So he wove a subtle web, in a little corner sly,
And set his table ready, to dine upon the Fly.
Then he came out to his door again, and merrily did sing,
'Come hither, hither, pretty Fly, with the pearl and silver wing;
Your robes are green and purple – there's a crest upon your head;
Your eyes are like the diamond bright, but mine are dull as lead!'

Alas, alas! how very soon this silly little Fly,
Hearing his wily, flattering words, came slowly flitting by;
With buzzing wings she hung aloft, then near and nearer drew,
Thinking only of her brilliant eyes, and green and purple hue –
Thinking only of her crested head – poor foolish thing! At last,
Up jumped the cunning Spider, and fiercely held her fast.
He dragged her up his winding stair, into his dismal den,

Within his little parlour – but she ne'er came out again!

And now dear little children, who may this story read,
To idle, silly flattering words, I pray you ne'er give heed:
Unto an evil counsellor, close heart and ear and eye,
 And take a lesson from this tale, of the Spider and the Fly.

Horace (Quintus Horatius Flaccus, 65 BC–8 BC)

O Fons Bandusiae (translated by A. S. Kline)

O Bandusian fountain, brighter than crystal,
worthy of sweet wine, not lacking in flowers,
tomorrow we'll honour you
with a kid, whose brow is budding

with those horns that are destined for love and battle.
All in vain: since this child of the playful herd will
darken your ice-cool waters,
with the stain of its crimson blood.

The implacable hour of the blazing dog-star
knows no way to touch you, you offer your lovely
coolness to bullocks, weary
of ploughing, and to wandering flocks.

And you too will be one of the famous fountains,
now I write of the holm oak that's rooted above
the cave in the rock where your
clear babbling waters run down.

TWO

'As I was young and easy under the apple boughs' – Childhood

I include here both poems about childhood and poems written for children, as the latter are often the first verses we hear and the ones we longest remember. Lewis Carroll's deliciously absurd poems were often based on the sort of improving verse that little Victorian girls like Alice would have had to learn by heart in their lessons, so it is rather lovely that his sillier versions are now some of the most familiar poems in English. 'Fern Hill' and the extract here included from Wordsworth's *Prelude* are two of the most beautiful evocations of the sheer exhilaration of tearing about the countryside ever written.

Thomas Hood (1799–1845)

I Remember, I Remember

I remember, I remember,
The house where I was born,
The little window where the sun
Came peeping in at morn;
He never came a wink too soon,
Nor brought too long a day;
But now, I often wish the night
Had borne my breath away.

I remember, I remember
The roses red and white,
The vi'lets and the lily-cups –
Those flowers made of light!
The lilacs where the robin built,
And where my brother set
The laburnum on his birthday, –
The tree is living yet!

I remember, I remember,
Where I was used to swing,
And thought the air must rush as fresh
To swallows on the wing;
My spirit flew in feathers then,
That is so heavy now,
And summer pools could hardly cool
The fever on my brow!

I remember, I remember,
The fir-trees dark and high;
I used to think their slender tops

Were close against the sky:
It was a childish ignorance,
But now 'tis little joy
To know I'm farther off from Heaven
Than when I was a boy.

Sylvia Plath (1932–63)

Morning Song

Love set you going like a fat gold watch.
The midwife slapped your footsoles, and your bald cry
Took its place among the elements.

Our voices echo, magnifying your arrival. New statue.
In a drafty museum, your nakedness
Shadows our safety. We stand round blankly as walls.

I'm no more your mother
Than the cloud that distills a mirror to reflect its own slow
Effacement at the wind's hand.

All night your moth-breath
Flickers among the flat pink roses. I wake to listen:
A far sea moves in my ear.

One cry, and I stumble from bed, cow-heavy and floral
In my Victorian nightgown.
Your mouth opens clean as a cat's. The window square

Whitens and swallows its dull stars. And now you try
Your handful of notes;
The clear vowels rise like balloons.

Edward Lear (1812–88)

The Pobble Who Has No Toes

The Pobble who has no toes
Had once as many as we;
When they said 'Some day you may lose them all;'
He replied 'Fish, fiddle-de-dee!'
And his Aunt Jobiska made him drink
Lavender water tinged with pink,
For she said 'The World in general knows
There's nothing so good for a Pobble's toes!'

The Pobble who has no toes
Swam across the Bristol Channel;
But before he set out he wrapped his nose
In a piece of scarlet flannel.
For his Aunt Jobiska said 'No harm
Can come to his toes if his nose is warm;
And it's perfectly known that a Pobble's toes
Are safe, – provided he minds his nose!'

The Pobble swam fast and well,
And when boats or ships came near him,
He tinkledy-blinkledy-winkled a bell,
So that all the world could hear him.
And all the Sailors and Admirals cried,
When they saw him nearing the further side –
'He has gone to fish for his Aunt Jobiska's
Runcible Cat with crimson whiskers!'

But before he touched the shore,
The shore of the Bristol Channel,
A sea-green porpoise carried away

His wrapper of scarlet flannel.
And when he came to observe his feet,
Formerly garnished with toes so neat,
His face at once became forlorn,
On perceiving that all his toes were gone!

And nobody ever knew,
From that dark day to the present,
Whoso had taken the Pobble's toes,
In a manner so far from pleasant.
Whether the shrimps, or crawfish grey,
Or crafty Mermaids stole them away –
Nobody knew: and nobody knows
How the Pobble was robbed of his twice five toes!

The Pobble who has no toes
Was placed in a friendly Bark,
And they rowed him back, and carried him up
To his Aunt Jobiska's Park.
And she made him a feast at his earnest wish
Of eggs and buttercups fried with fish, –
And she said 'It's a fact the whole world knows,
That Pobbles are happier without their toes!'

William Wordsworth (1770–1850)

The Prelude [extract]

And in the frosty season, when the sun
Was set, and visible for many a mile
The cottage windows blazed through the twilight gloom,
I heeded not their summons: happy time
It was indeed for all of us – for me
It was a time of rapture! Clear and loud
The village clock tolled six; I wheeled about
Proud and exulting, like an untired horse
That cares not for his home. All shod with steel
We hissed along the polished ice in games
Confederate, imitative of the chase
And woodland pleasures – the resounding horn,
The pack loud chiming, and the hunted hare.
So through the darkness and the cold we flew,
And not a voice was idle; with the din
Smitten, the precipices rang aloud;
The leafless trees and every icy crag
Tinkled like iron; while the distant hills
Into the tumult sent an alien sound
Of melancholy, not unnoticed, while the stars,
Eastward, were sparkling clear, and in the west
The orange sky of evening died away.

Not seldom from the uproar I retired
Into a silent bay, or sportively
Glanced sideway, leaving the tumultuous throng,
To cut across the reflex of a star
That fled, and, flying still before me, gleamed
Upon the glassy plain; and oftentimes

When we had given our bodies to the wind,
And all the shadowy banks on either side
Came sweeping through the darkness, spinning still
The rapid line of motion, then at once
Have I, reclining back upon my heels,
Stopped short; yet still the solitary cliffs
Wheeled by me – even as if the earth had rolled
With visible motion her diurnal round!
Behind me did they stretch in solemn train,
Feebler and feebler, and I stood and watched
Till all was tranquil as a dreamless sleep.

Hilaire Belloc (1870–1953)

Jim
Who ran away from his Nurse and was eaten by a Lion

There was a Boy whose name was Jim;
His Friends were very good to him.
They gave him Tea, and Cakes, and Jam,
And slices of delicious Ham,
And Chocolate with pink inside
And little Tricycles to ride,
And read him Stories through and through,
And even took him to the Zoo –
But there it was the dreadful Fate
Befell him, which I now relate.

You know – or at least you ought to know,
For I have often told you so –
That Children never are allowed
To leave their Nurses in a Crowd;
Now this was Jim's especial Foible,

He ran away when he was able,
And on this inauspicious day
He slipped his hand and ran away!

He hadn't gone a yard when – Bang!
With open Jaws, a lion sprang,
And hungrily began to eat
The Boy: beginning at his feet.
Now, just imagine how it feels
When first your toes and then your heels,
And then by gradual degrees,
Your shins and ankles, calves and knees,
Are slowly eaten, bit by bit.
No wonder Jim detested it!
No wonder that he shouted 'Hi!'

The Honest Keeper heard his cry,
Though very fat he almost ran
To help the little gentleman.
'Ponto!' he ordered as he came
(For Ponto was the Lion's name),
'Ponto!' he cried, with angry Frown,
'Let go, Sir! Down, Sir! Put it down!'
The Lion made a sudden stop,
He let the Dainty Morsel drop,
And slunk reluctant to his Cage,
Snarling with Disappointed Rage.
But when he bent him over Jim,
The Honest Keeper's eyes were dim.
The Lion having reached his Head,
The Miserable Boy was dead!

When Nurse informed his Parents, they
Were more Concerned than I can say:–

His Mother, as She dried her eyes,
Said, 'Well – it gives me no surprise,
He would not do as he was told!'
His Father, who was self-controlled,
Bade all the children round attend
To James's miserable end,
And always keep a-hold of Nurse
For fear of finding something worse.

Lewis Carroll (1832–98)

You Are Old, Father William

'You are old, Father William,' the young man said
  'And your hair has become very white;
And yet you incessantly stand on your head –
  Do you think, at your age, it is right?'

'In my youth', Father William replied to his son,
  'I feared it might injure the brain;
But, now that I'm perfectly sure I have none,
  Why, I do it again and again.'

'You are old', said the youth, 'as I mentioned before,
  And have grown most uncommonly fat;
Yet you turned a back-somersault in at the door –
  Pray, what is the reason of that?'

'In my youth', said the sage, as he shook his grey locks,
  'I kept all my limbs very supple
By the use of this ointment – one shilling the box –
  Allow me to sell you a couple?'

'You are old', said the youth, 'and your jaws are too weak
  For anything tougher than suet;

Yet you finished the goose, with the bones and the beak –
  Pray, how did you manage to do it?'

'In my youth', said his father, 'I took to the law,
  And argued each case with my wife;
And the muscular strength, which it gave to my jaw,
  Has lasted the rest of my life.'

'You are old', said the youth, 'one would hardly suppose
  That your eye was as steady as ever;
Yet you balanced an eel on the end of your nose –
  What made you so awfully clever?'

'I have answered three questions, and that is enough,'
  Said his father, 'don't give yourself airs!
Do you think I can listen all day to such stuff?
  Be off, or I'll kick you downstairs!'

The Walrus and the Carpenter

The sun was shining on the sea,
Shining with all his might:
He did his very best to make
The billows smooth and bright –
And this was odd, because it was
The middle of the night.

The moon was shining sulkily,
Because she thought the sun
Had got no business to be there
After the day was done –
'It's very rude of him,' she said,
'To come and spoil the fun!'

The sea was wet as wet could be,
The sands were dry as dry.
You could not see a cloud, because
No cloud was in the sky:
No birds were flying overhead –
There were no birds to fly.

The Walrus and the Carpenter
Were walking close at hand;
They wept like anything to see
Such quantities of sand:
'If this were only cleared away,'
They said, 'it would be grand!'

'If seven maids with seven mops
Swept it for half a year.
Do you suppose,' the Walrus said,
'That they could get it clear?'
'I doubt it,' said the Carpenter,
And shed a bitter tear.

'O Oysters, come and walk with us!'
The Walrus did beseech.
'A pleasant walk, a pleasant talk,
Along the briny beach:
We cannot do with more than four,
To give a hand to each.'

The eldest Oyster looked at him,
But never a word he said:
The eldest Oyster winked his eye,
And shook his heavy head –
Meaning to say he did not choose
To leave the oyster-bed.

But four young Oysters hurried up,
All eager for the treat:
Their coats were brushed, their faces washed,
Their shoes were clean and neat –
And this was odd, because, you know,
They hadn't any feet.

Four other Oysters followed them,
And yet another four;
And thick and fast they came at last,
And more, and more, and more –
All hopping through the frothy waves,
And scrambling to the shore.

The Walrus and the Carpenter
Walked on a mile or so,
And then they rested on a rock
Conveniently low:
And all the little Oysters stood
And waited in a row.

'The time has come,' the Walrus said,
'To talk of many things:
Of shoes – and ships – and sealing-wax –
Of cabbages – and kings –
And why the sea is boiling hot –
And whether pigs have wings.'

'But wait a bit,' the Oysters cried,
'Before we have our chat;
For some of us are out of breath,
And all of us are fat!'
'No hurry!' said the Carpenter.
They thanked him much for that.

'A loaf of bread,' the Walrus said,
'Is what we chiefly need:
Pepper and vinegar besides
Are very good indeed –
Now if you're ready, Oysters dear,
We can begin to feed.'

'But not on us!' the Oysters cried,
Turning a little blue.
'After such kindness, that would be
A dismal thing to do!'
'The night is fine,' the Walrus said.
'Do you admire the view?

'It was so kind of you to come!
And you are very nice!'
The Carpenter said nothing but
'Cut us another slice:
I wish you were not quite so deaf –
I've had to ask you twice!'

'It seems a shame,' the Walrus said,
'To play them such a trick,
After we've brought them out so far,
And made them trot so quick!'
The Carpenter said nothing but
'The butter's spread too thick!'

'I weep for you,' the Walrus said:
'I deeply sympathize.'
With sobs and tears he sorted out
Those of the largest size,
Holding his pocket-handkerchief
Before his streaming eyes.

'O Oysters,' said the Carpenter,
'You've had a pleasant run!
Shall we be trotting home again?'
But answer came there none –
And this was scarcely odd, because
They'd eaten every one.

Dylan Thomas (1914–53)

Fern Hill

Now as I was young and easy under the apple boughs
About the lilting house and happy as the grass was green,
   The night above the dingle starry,
     Time let me hail and climb
   Golden in the heyday of his eyes,
And honoured among wagons I was prince of the apple towns
And once below a time I lordly had the trees and leaves
     Trail with daisies and barley
   Down the rivers of the windfall light.

And as I was green and carefree, famous among the barns
About the happy yard and singing as the farm was home,
   In the sun that is young once only,
     Time let me play and be
   Golden in the mercy of his means,
And green and golden I was huntsman and herdsman, the calves
Sang to my horn, the foxes on the hills barked clear and cold,
     And the sabbath rang slowly
   In the pebbles of the holy streams.

All the sun long it was running, it was lovely, the hay
Fields high as the house, the tunes from the chimneys, it was air

And playing, lovely and watery
    And fire green as grass.
And nightly under the simple stars
As I rode to sleep the owls were bearing the farm away,
All the moon long I heard, blessed among stables, the nightjars
    Flying with the ricks, and the horses
        Flashing into the dark.

And then to awake, and the farm, like a wanderer white
With the dew, come back, the cock on his shoulder: it, was all
    Shining, it was Adam and maiden,
        The sky gathered again
    And the sun grew round that very day.
So it must have been after the birth of the simple light
In the first, spinning place, the spellbound horses walking warm
    Out of the whinnying green stable
        On to the fields of praise.

And honoured among foxes and pheasants by the gay house
Under the new made clouds and happy as the heart was long,
    In the sun born over and over,
        I ran my heedless ways,
    My wishes raced through the house high hay
And nothing I cared, at my sky blue trades, that time allows
In all his tuneful turning so few and such morning songs
    Before the children green and golden
        Follow him out of grace,

Nothing I cared, in the lamb white days, that time would take me
Up to the swallow thronged loft by the shadow of my hand,
    In the moon that is always rising,
        Nor that riding to sleep
    I should hear him fly with the high fields
And wake to the farm forever fled from the childless land.

Oh as I was young and easy in the mercy of his means,
    Time held me green and dying
  Though I sang in my chains like the sea.

A. A. Milne (1882–1956)

The King's Breakfast

The King asked
The Queen, and
The Queen asked
The Dairymaid:
'Could we have some butter for
The Royal slice of bread?'
The Queen asked the Dairymaid,
The Dairymaid
Said, 'Certainly,
I'll go and tell the cow
Now
Before she goes to bed.'

The Dairymaid
She curtsied,
And went and told
The Alderney:
'Don't forget the butter for
The Royal slice of bread.'
The Alderney
Said sleepily:
'You'd better tell
His Majesty
That many people nowadays

Like marmalade
Instead.'

The Dairymaid
Said, 'Fancy!'
And went to
Her Majesty.
She curtsied to the Queen, and
She turned a little red:
'Excuse me,
Your Majesty,
For taking of
The liberty,
But marmalade is tasty, if
It's very
Thickly
Spread.'

The Queen said
'Oh!:
And went to
His Majesty:
'Talking of the butter for
The royal slice of bread,
Many people
Think that
Marmalade
Is nicer.
Would you like to try a little
Marmalade
Instead?'

The King said,
'Bother!'

And then he said,
'Oh, deary me!'
The King sobbed, 'Oh, deary me!'
And went back to bed.
'Nobody,'
He whimpered,
'Could call me
A fussy man;
I only want
A little bit
Of butter for
My bread!'

The Queen said,
'There, there!'
And went to
The Dairymaid.
The Dairymaid
Said, 'There, there!'
And went to the shed.
The cow said,
'There, there!
I didn't really
Mean it;
Here's milk for his porringer,
And butter for his bread.'

The Queen took
The butter
And brought it to
His Majesty;
The King said,
'Butter, eh?'

And bounced out of bed.
'Nobody,' he said,
As he kissed her
Tenderly,
'Nobody,' he said,
As he slid down the banisters,
'Nobody,
My darling,
Could call me
A fussy man –
BUT
I do like a little bit of butter to my bread!'

Allan Ahlberg (1938–)

Scissors

Nobody leave the room.
Everyone listen to me.
We had ten-pair of scissors
At half-past two,
 And now there's only three.

Seven pair of scissors,
Disappeared from sight.
Not one of you leaves
Till we find them.
We can stop here all night!

Scissors don't lose themselves,
 Melt away, or explode.
Scissors have not got

Legs of their own
To go running off up the road.

We really need those scissors,
That's what makes me mad.
If it was seven pairs
Of children we'd lost,
It wouldn't be so bad.

I don't want to hear excuses.
Don't anyone speak.
Just ransack this room
Till we find them,
Or we'll stop here . . . all week!

THREE

'We returned to our places, these kingdoms' – Home and Abroad

The themes of voyage and return have occupied the bards since the earliest times. The question they pose is: what influence does our home turf – be it distant Africa or Scotland – have on our characters, and how do our wanderings shape us? The lure of home is like a siren's call to the traveller though, as poets often observe, just as Eliot does in 'The Journey of the Magi', there may be no possibility of true homecoming once the voyage has changed everything.

Anonymous

Sir Patrick Spens

The king sits in Dumferline town
Drinking the blude-reid wine:
'O whar will I get a guid sailor
To sail this ship of mine?'

Up and spak an eldern knicht,
Sat at the king's richt knee:
'Sir Patrick Spens is the best sailor
That sails upon the sea.'

The king has written a braid letter
And signed it wi' his hand,
And sent it to Sir Patrick Spens,
Was walking on the sand.

The first line that Sir Patrick read
A loud lauch lauched he;
The next line that Sir Patrick read,
The tear blinded his ee.

'O wha is this has done this deed,
This ill deed done to me,
To send me out this time o'the year,
To sail upon the sea?

'Mak haste, mak haste, my mirry men all,
Our guid ship sails the morn.'
'O say na sae, my master dear,
For I fear a deadly storm.'

'Late, late yestre'en I saw the new moon
Wi' the auld moon in hir arm,

And I fear, I fear, my dear master,
That we will come to harm.'

O our Scots nobles were richt laith
To weet their cork-heeled shoon,
But lang or a' the play were played
Their hats they swam aboon.

O lang, lang may their ladies sit,
Wi' their fans into their hand,
Or ere they see Sir Patrick Spens
Come sailing to the land.

O lang, lang may the ladies stand
Wi' their gold kems in their hair,
Waiting for their ain dear lords,
For they'll see them na mair.

Half o'er, half o'er to Aberdour
It's fifty fadom deep,
And there lies guid Sir Patrick Spens
Wi' the Scots lords at his feet.

(*braid* – broad: in this sense perhaps a long letter, or one meant to be read in public; *laith* – loath; *shoon* – shoes; *kems* – combs; *fadom* – fathoms)

'Banjo' (Andrew Barton) Paterson (1864–1941)

Waltzing Matilda (Carrying a Swag)

Oh! there once was a swagman camped in a Billabong,
Under the shade of a Coolabah tree;
And he sang as he looked at his old billy boiling,

'Who'll come a-waltzing Matilda with me?'

Who'll come a-waltzing Matilda, my darling,
Who'll come a-waltzing Matilda with me?
Waltzing Matilda and leading a water-bag –
Who'll come a-waltzing Matilda with me?

Down came a jumbuck to drink at the water-hole,
Up jumped the swagman and grabbed him in glee;
And he sang as he stowed him away in his tucker-bag
You'll come a-waltzing Matilda with me.'

Who'll come a-waltzing Matilda, my darling,
Who'll come a-waltzing Matilda with me?
Waltzing Matilda and leading a water-bag –
Who'll come a-waltzing Matilda with me?

Down came the Squatter a-riding his thoroughbred;
Down came Policemen – one, two and three.
'Whose is the jumbuck you've got in the tucker-bag?
You'll come a-waltzing Matilda with me.'

Who'll come a-waltzing Matilda, my darling,
Who'll come a-waltzing Matilda with me?
Waltzing Matilda and leading a water-bag –
Who'll come a-waltzing Matilda with me?

But the swagman, he up and jumped in the water-hole,
Drowning himself by the Coolabah tree;
And his ghost may be heard as it sings in the Billabong
'Who'll come a-waltzing Matilda with me?'

Who'll come a-waltzing Matilda, my darling,
Who'll come a-waltzing Matilda with me?
Waltzing Matilda and leading a water-bag –
Who'll come a-waltzing Matilda with me?

T. S. Eliot (1888–1965)

The Journey of the Magi

'A cold coming we had of it,
Just the worst time of the year
For a journey, and such a long journey:
The ways deep and the weather sharp,
The very dead of winter.'
And the camels galled, sore-footed, refractory,
Lying down in the melting snow.
There were times when we regretted
The summer palaces on slopes, the terraces,
And the silken girls bringing sherbet.
Then the camel men cursing and grumbling
And running away, and wanting their liquor and women,
And the night-fires going out, and the lack of shelters,
And the cities hostile and the towns unfriendly
And the villages dirty and charging high prices:
A hard time we had of it.
At the end we preferred to travel all night,
Sleeping in snatches,
With the voices singing in our ears, saying
That this was all folly.

Then at dawn we came down to a temperate valley,
Wet, below the snow line, smelling of vegetation;
With a running stream and a water-mill beating the darkness,
And three trees on the low sky,
And an old white horse galloped away in the meadow.
Then we came to a tavern with vine-leaves over the lintel,
Six hands at an open door dicing for pieces of silver,
And feet kicking the empty wineskins.

But there was no information, and so we continued
And arrived at evening, not a moment too soon
Finding the place; it was (you may say) satisfactory.

All this was a long time ago, I remember,
And I would do it again, but set down
This set down
This: were we led all that way for
Birth or Death? There was a Birth, certainly,
We had evidence and no doubt. I had seen birth and death,
But had thought they were different; this Birth was
Hard and bitter agony for us, like Death, our death.
We returned to our places, these Kingdoms,
But no longer at ease here, in the old dispensation,
With an alien people clutching their gods.
I should be glad of another death.

Sir Walter Scott (1771–1832)

The Rover

A weary lot is thine, fair maid,
A weary lot is thine!
To pull the thorn thy brow to braid,
And press the rue for wine.
A lightsome eye, a soldier's mien
A feather of the blue,
A doublet of the Lincoln green –
No more of me you knew
My Love!
No more of me you knew.

'This morn is merry June, I trow,

The rose is budding fain;
But she shall bloom in winter snow
Ere we two meet again.'
He turn'd his charger as he spake
Upon the river shore,
He gave the bridle-reins a shake,
Said 'Adieu for evermore.
My Love!
And adieu for evermore.'

Derek Walcott (1930–2017)

A Far Cry from Africa

A wind is ruffling the tawny pelt
Of Africa. Kikuyu, quick as flies,
Batten upon the bloodstreams of the veldt.
Corpses are scattered through a paradise.
Only the worm, colonel of carrion, cries:
'Waste no compassion on these separate dead!'
Statistics justify and scholars seize
The salients of colonial policy.
What is that to the white child hacked in bed?
To savages, expendable as Jews?

Threshed out by beaters, the long rushes break
In a white dust of ibises whose cries
Have wheeled since civilization's dawn
From the parched river or beast-teeming plain.
The violence of beast on beast is read
As natural law, but upright man
Seeks his divinity by inflicting pain.

Delirious as these worried beasts, his wars
Dance to the tightened carcass of a drum,
While he calls courage still that native dread
Of the white peace contracted by the dead.

Again brutish necessity wipes its hands
Upon the napkin of a dirty cause, again
A waste of our compassion, as with Spain,
The gorilla wrestles with the superman.
I who am poisoned with the blood of both,
Where shall I turn, divided to the vein?
I who have cursed
The drunken officer of British rule, how choose
Between this Africa and the English tongue I love?
Betray them both, or give back what they give?
How can I face such slaughter and be cool?
How can I turn from Africa and live?

Edward Lear (1812–88)

The Jumblies

I

They went to sea in a Sieve, they did,
In a Sieve they went to sea:
In spite of all their friends could say,
On a winter's morn, on a stormy day,
In a Sieve they went to sea!
And when the Sieve turned round and round,
And every one cried, 'You'll all be drowned!'
They called aloud, 'Our Sieve ain't big,
But we don't care a button! we don't care a fig!

In a Sieve we'll go to sea!'
    Far and few, far and few,
    Are the lands where the Jumblies live;
    Their heads are green, and their hands are blue,
    And they went to sea in a Sieve.

II

They sailed away in a Sieve, they did,
In a Sieve they sailed so fast,
With only a beautiful pea-green veil
Tied with a riband by way of a sail,
To a small tobacco-pipe mast;
And every one said, who saw them go,
'O won't they be soon upset, you know!
For the sky is dark, and the voyage is long,
And happen what may, it's extremely wrong
In a Sieve to sail so fast!'
    Far and few, far and few,
    Are the lands where the Jumblies live;
    Their heads are green, and their hands are blue,
    And they went to sea in a Sieve.

III

The water it soon came in, it did,
The water it soon came in;
So to keep them dry, they wrapped their feet
In a pinky paper all folded neat,
And they fastened it down with a pin.
And they passed the night in a crockery-jar,
And each of them said, 'How wise we are!
Though the sky be dark, and the voyage be long,
Yet we never can think we were rash or wrong,

While round in our Sieve we spin!'
    Far and few, far and few,
    Are the lands where the Jumblies live;
    Their heads are green, and their hands are blue,
    And they went to sea in a Sieve.

IV

And all night long they sailed away;
And when the sun went down,
They whistled and warbled a moony song
To the echoing sound of a coppery gong,
In the shade of the mountains brown.
'O Timballo! How happy we are,
When we live in a sieve and a crockery-jar,
And all night long in the moonlight pale,
We sail away with a pea-green sail,
In the shade of the mountains brown!'
    Far and few, far and few,
    Are the lands where the Jumblies live;
    Their heads are green, and their hands are blue,
    And they went to sea in a Sieve.

V

They sailed to the Western Sea, they did,
To a land all covered with trees,
And they bought an Owl, and a useful Cart,
And a pound of Rice, and a Cranberry Tart,
And a hive of silvery Bees.
And they bought a Pig, and some green Jack-daws,
And a lovely Monkey with lollipop paws,
And forty bottles of Ring-Bo-Ree,
And no end of Stilton Cheese.

Far and few, far and few,
Are the lands where the Jumblies live;
Their heads are green, and their hands are blue,
And they went to sea in a Sieve.

VI

And in twenty years they all came back,
In twenty years or more,
And every one said, 'How tall they've grown!'
For they've been to the Lakes, and the Torrible Zone,
And the hills of the Chankly Bore!'
And they drank their health, and gave them a feast
Of dumplings made of beautiful yeast;
And everyone said, 'If we only live,
We too will go to sea in a Sieve –
To the hills of the Chankly Bore!'
Far and few, far and few,
Are the lands where the Jumblies live;
Their heads are green, and their hands are blue,
And they went to sea in a Sieve.

Hugh MacDiarmid (1892–1978)

A Drunk Man Looks at the Thistle [extract]

The language that but sparely flooers
And maistly gangs to weed;
The thocht o Christ and Calvary
Aye likkenin in my heid;
And aa the dour provincial thocht
That merks the Scottish breed
– These are the thistle's characters,

To argie there's nae need.
Hoo weel my verse embodies
The thistle you can read!
– But will a Scotsman never
Frae this vile growth be freed?...

(*flooers* – flowers; *maistly* – mostly; *likkenin* – possibly 'going round in')

Alfred, Lord Tennyson (1809–92)

The Lotos Eaters [extract]

'Courage!' he said, and pointed toward the land,
'This mounting wave will roll us shoreward soon.'
In the afternoon they came unto a land,
In which it seemed always afternoon.
All round the coast the languid air did swoon,
Breathing like one that hath a weary dream.
Full-faced above the valley stood the moon;
And like a downward smoke, the slender stream
Along the cliff to fall and pause and fall did seem.

A land of streams! some, like a downward smoke,
Slow-dropping veils of thinnest lawn, did go;
And some through wavering lights and shadows broke,
Rolling a slumbrous sheet of foam below.
They saw the gleaming river seaward flow
From the inner land: far off, three mountain-tops,
Three silent pinnacles of aged snow,
Stood sunset-flushed: and, dewed with showery drops,
Up-clomb the shadowy pine above the woven copse.

The charmed sunset lingered low adown
In the red West: through mountain clefts the dale
Was seen far inland, and the yellow down
Bordered with palm, and many a winding vale
And meadow, set with slender galingale;
A land where all things always seemed the same!
And round about the keel with faces pale,
Dark faces pale against that rosy flame,
The mild-eyed melancholy Lotos-eaters came.

Branches they bore of that enchanted stem,
Laden with flower and fruit, whereof they gave
To each, but whoso did receive of them,
And taste, to him the gushing of the wave
Far far away did seem to mourn and rave
On alien shores; and if his fellow spake,
His voice was thin, as voices from the grave;
And deep-asleep he seemed, yet all awake,
And music in his ears his beating heart did make.

They sat them down upon the yellow sand,
Between the sun and moon upon the shore;
And sweet it was to dream of Fatherland,
Of child, and wife, and slave; but evermore
Most weary seemed the sea, weary the oar,
Weary the wandering fields of barren foam.
Then some one said, 'We will return no more';
And all at once they sang, 'Our island home
Is far beyond the wave; we will no longer roam.'

FOUR

'An angel writing in a book of gold' – Talking to Gods

From hymns of praise, through rhythmic wrestling with doubt, to prescriptions for a well-lived and godly life, religion has inspired a vast range of verses. These verses span several centuries, but each addresses the eternal question of man's relationship with his maker. Throughout history many clergymen – George Herbert and John Donne, for example – have also been writers, and have felt the need to engage with the divine through language.

Christina Rossetti (1830–94)

Up-Hill

Does the road wind up-hill all the way?
Yes, to the very end.
Will the day's journey take the whole long day?
From morn to night, my friend.

But is there for the night a resting-place?
A roof for when the slow dark hours begin.
May not the darkness hide it from my face?
You cannot miss that inn.

Shall I meet other wayfarers at night?
Those who have gone before.
Then must I knock, or call when just in sight?
They will not keep you standing at that door.

Shall I find comfort, travel-sore and weak?
Of labour you shall find the sum.
Will there be beds for me and all who seek?
Yea, beds for all who come.

George Herbert (1593–1633)

The Elixir

Teach me, my God and King,
In all things thee to see,
And what I do in anything
To do it as for thee.

Not rudely, as a beast,
To run into an action;
But still to make thee prepossest,
And give it his perfection.

A man that looks on glass,
On it may stay his eye,
Or, if he pleaseth, through it pass,
And then the heaven espy.

All may of thee partake:
Nothing can be so mean
Which with his tincture – *'for thy sake'* –
Will not grow bright and clean.

A servant with this clause
Makes drudgery divine:
Who sweeps a room as for thy laws,
Makes that and th' action fine.

This is the famous stone
That turneth all to gold;
For that which God doth touch and own
Cannot for less be told.

Leigh Hunt (1784–1859)

Abou Ben Adhem

Abou Ben Adhem (may his tribe increase!)
Awoke one night from a deep dream of peace,
And saw, within the moonlight in his room,
Making it rich, and like a lily in bloom,
An angel writing in a book of gold:–

Exceeding peace had made Ben Adhem bold,
And to the Presence in the room he said
'What writest thou?' – The vision raised its head,
And with a look made of all sweet accord,
Answered 'The names of those who love the Lord.'
'And is mine one?' said Abou. 'Nay, not so,'
Replied the angel. Abou spoke more low,
But cheerly still, and said 'I pray thee, then,
Write me as one that loves his fellow men.'

The angel wrote, and vanished. The next night
It came again with a great wakening light,
And showed the names whom love of God had blessed,
And lo! Ben Adhem's name led all the rest.

Emily Brontë (1818–48)

No Coward Soul Is Mine

No coward soul is mine,
No trembler in the world's storm-troubled sphere!
I see Heaven's glories shine,
And Faith shines equal, arming me from Fear.

O God within my breast,
Almighty, ever-present Deity!
Life, that in me hast rest,
As I, undying Life, have power in Thee!

Vain are the thousand creeds
That move men's hearts: unutterably vain;
Worthless as withered weeds,
Or idlest froth amid the boundless main,

To waken doubt in one
Holding so fast by thy infinity,
So surely anchored on
The steadfast rock of Immortality.

With wide-embracing love
Thy spirit animates eternal years,
Pervades and broods above,
Changes, sustains, dissolves, creates, and rears.

Though earth and moon were gone,
And suns and universes ceased to be,
And thou were left alone,
Every existence would exist in Thee.

There is not room for Death,
Nor atom that his might could render void:
Since thou art Being and Breath,
And what Thou art may never be destroyed.

Henry Vaughan (1621–95)

They Are All Gone into the World of Light

They are all gone into the world of light!
And I alone sit ling'ring here;
Their very memory is fair and bright,
And my sad thoughts doth clear.

It glows and glitters in my cloudy breast
Like stars upon some gloomy grove,
Or those faint beams in which this hill is dressed,
After the sun's remove.

I see them walking in an air of glory,
Whose light doth trample on my days;
My days, which are at best but dull and hoary,
Mere glimmering and decays.

O holy hope! and high humility,
High as the heavens above!
These are your walks, and you have showed them me
To kindle my cold love.

Dear, beauteous death! the jewel of the just,
Shining nowhere, but in the dark;
What mysteries do lie beyond thy dust,
Could man outlook that mark!

He that hath found some fledged bird's nest, may know
At first sight, if the bird be flown;
But what fair well, or grove he sings in now,
That is to him unknown.

And yet, as angels in some brighter dreams
Call to the soul, when man doth sleep,
So some strange thoughts transcend our wonted themes,
And into glory peep.

If a star were confined into a tomb
Her captive flames must needs burn there;
But when the hand that locked her up, gives room,
She'll shine through all the sphere.

O Father of eternal life, and all
Created glories under Thee!
Resume thy spirit from this world of thrall
Into true liberty.

Either disperse these mists, which blot and fill
My perspective still as they pass;
Or else remove me hence unto that hill,
Where I shall need no glass.

Robert Graves (1895–1985)

In the Wilderness

Christ of His gentleness
Thirsting and hungering
Walked in the wilderness;
Soft words of grace He spoke
Unto lost desert-folk
That listened wondering.
He heard the bitterns call
From the ruined palace-wall,
Answered them brotherly.
He held communion
With the she-pelican
Of lonely piety.
Basilisk, cockatrice,
Flocked to his homilies,
With mail of dread device,
With monstrous barbèd slings,
With eager dragon-eyes;
Great rats on leather wings,
And poor blind broken things,
Foul in their miseries.
And ever with Him went,
Of all His wanderings
Comrade, with ragged coat,

Gaunt ribs – poor innocent –
Bleeding foot, burning throat,
The guileless old scapegoat;
For forty nights and days
Followed in Jesus' ways,
Sure guard behind Him kept,
Tears like a lover wept.

John Betjeman (1906–84)

Diary of a Church Mouse

Here among long-discarded cassocks,
Damp stools, and half-split open hassocks,
Here where the Vicar never looks
I nibble through old service books.
Lean and alone I spend my days
Behind this Church of England baize.
I share my dark forgotten room
With two oil-lamps and half a broom.
The cleaner never bothers me,
So here I eat my frugal tea.
My bread is sawdust mixed with straw;
My jam is polish for the floor.
Christmas and Easter may be feasts
For congregations and for priests,
And so may Whitsun. All the same,
They do not fill my meagre frame.
For me the only feast at all
Is Autumn's Harvest Festival,
When I can satisfy my want
With ears of corn around the font.

I climb the eagle's brazen head
To burrow through a loaf of bread.
I scramble up the pulpit stair
And gnaw the marrows hanging there.
It is enjoyable to taste
These items ere they go to waste,
But how annoying when one finds
That other mice with pagan minds
Come into church my food to share
Who have no proper business there.
Two field mice who have no desire
To be baptized, invade the choir.
A large and most unfriendly rat
Comes in to see what we are at.
He says he thinks there is no God
And yet he comes… it's rather odd.
This year he stole a sheaf of wheat
(It screened our special preacher's seat),
And prosperous mice from fields away
Come in to hear the organ play,
And under cover of its notes
Ate through the altar's sheaf of oats.
A Low Church mouse, who thinks that I
Am too papistical, and High,
Yet somehow doesn't think it wrong
To munch through Harvest Evensong,
While I, who starve the whole year through,
Must share my food with rodents who
Except at this time of the year
Not once inside the church appear.
Within the human world I know
Such goings-on could not be so,

For human beings only do
What their religion tells them to.
They read the Bible every day
And always, night and morning, pray,
And just like me, the good church mouse,
Worship each week in God's own house,
But all the same it's strange to me
How very full the church can be
With people I don't see at all
Except at Harvest Festival.

John Gillespie Magee (1922–41)

High Flight

Oh! I have slipped the surly bonds of Earth
And danced the skies on laughter-silvered wings;
Sunward I've climbed, and joined the tumbling mirth
Of sun-split clouds, – and done a hundred things
You have not dreamed of – wheeled and soared and swung
High in the sunlit silence. Hov'ring there,
I've chased the shouting wind along, and flung
My eager craft through footless halls of air . . .

Up, up the long, delirious burning blue
I've topped the wind-swept heights with easy grace
Where never lark, or ever eagle flew –
And, while with silent, lifting mind I've trod
The high untrespassed sanctity of space,
Put out my hand, and touched the face of God.

Max Ehrmann (1872–1945)

Desiderata

Go placidly amid the noise and the haste, and remember
what peace there may be in silence. As far as possible without
surrender be on good terms with all persons.

Speak your truth quietly and clearly; and listen to others, even to
the dull and the ignorant, they too have their story. Avoid loud
and aggressive persons, they are vexations to the spirit.

If you compare yourself to others, you may become vain and
bitter; for always there will be greater and lesser persons than
yourself.

Enjoy your achievements as well as your plans. Keep interested
in your own career, however humble; it is a real possession in the
changing fortunes of time.

Exercise caution in your business affairs, for the the world is
full of trickery. But let not this blind you to what virtue there is;
many persons strive for high ideals, and everywhere life is full of
heroism.

Be yourself. Especially do not feign affection. Neither be cynical
about love; for in the face of all aridity and disenchantment it is
as perennial as the grass. Take kindly the counsel of the years,
gracefully surrendering the things of youth.

Nurture strength of spirit to shield you in sudden misfortune.
But do not distress yourself with dark imaginings. Many fears are
born of fatigue and loneliness.

Beyond a wholesome discipline, be gentle with yourself. You are
a child of the universe, no less than the trees and the stars; you

have a right to be here. And whether or not it is clear to you, no doubt the universe is unfolding as it should.

Therefore, be at peace with God, whatever you conceive him to be, and whatever your labours and aspirations in the noisy confusion of life, keep peace in your soul. With all its sham, drudgery and broken dreams, it is still a beautiful world.

Be cheerful. Strive to be happy.

FIVE

'Two hearts beating each to each' – Love

Probably the most popular subject of all for poetry is, of course, the endless human conundrum of love. From the flush and flutter of first attraction, whether passionately returned or hopelessly unrequited, love's many splendours – and miseries – provide endless inspiration. So here are pragmatic lovers, who admit their lovers' faults, as well as those who have been deserted like Matthew Arnold's bereft merman. Here are warnings for the young and memories for the old, and tales of the loves that end well – as well as those that don't.

William Shakespeare (1564–1616)

Sonnet 73

That time of year thou mayst in me behold
When yellow leaves, or none, or few, do hang
Upon those boughs which shake against the cold,
Bare ruin'd choirs, where late the sweet birds sang.
In me thou see'st the twilight of such day
As after sunset fadeth in the west,
Which by and by black night doth take away,
Death's second self; that seals up all in rest.
In me thou see'st the glowing of such fire,
That on the ashes of his youth doth lie,
As the death-bed, whereon it must expire,
Consum'd with that which it was nourish'd by.
  This thou perceiv'st, which makes thy love more strong,
  To love that well, which thou must leave ere long.

Sonnet 130

My mistress' eyes are nothing like the sun;
Coral is far more red than her lips' red;
If snow be white, why then her breasts are dun:
If hairs be wires, black wires grow on her head:
I have seen roses damasked, red and white,
But no such roses see I in her cheeks;
And in some perfumes is there more delight
Than in the breath that from my mistress reeks.
I love to hear her speak, yet well I know,
That music hath a far more pleasing sound:
I grant I never saw a goddess go,

My mistress, when she walks, treads on the ground.
   And yet by heaven I think my love as rare,
   As any she belied with false compare.

Philip Larkin (1922–85)

An Arundel Tomb

Side by side, their faces blurred,
The earl and countess lie in stone,
Their proper habits vaguely shown
As jointed armour, stiffened pleat,
And that faint hint of the absurd —
The little dogs under their feet.

Such plainness of the pre-baroque
Hardly involves the eye, until
It meets his left-hand gauntlet, still
Clasped empty in the other; and
One sees, with a sharp tender shock
His hand withdrawn, holding her hand.

They would not think to lie so long.
Such faithfulness in effigy
Was just a detail friends would see:
A sculptor's sweet commissioned grace
Thrown off in helping to prolong
The Latin names around the base.

They would not guess how early in
Their supine stationary voyage
The air would change to soundless damage,
Turn the old tenantry away;

How soon succeeding eyes begin
To look, not read. Rigidly they

Persisted, linked, through lengths and breadths
Of time. Snow fell, undated. Light
Each summer thronged the glass. A bright
Litter of birdcalls strewed the same
Bone-riddled ground. And up the paths
The endless altered people came,

Washing at their identity.
Now, helpless in the hollow of
An unarmorial age, a trough
Of smoke in slow suspended skeins
Above their scrap of history,
Only an attitude remains:

Time has transfigured them into
Untruth. The stone fidelity
They hardly meant has come to be
Their final blazon, and to prove
Our almost-instinct almost true:
What will survive of us is love.

John Clare (1793–1864)

Song ['I hid my love when young while I']

I hid my love when young while I
Couldn't bear the buzzing of a fly
I hid my love to my despite
Till I could not bear to look at light
I dare not gaze upon her face
But left her memory in each place

Where ere I saw a wild flower lie
I kissed and bade my love goodbye

I met her in the greenest dells
Where dew drops pearl the wood bluebells
The lost breeze kissed her bright blue eye
The bee kissed and went singing by
A sunbeam found a passage there
A gold chain round her neck so fair
As secret as the wild bee's song
She lay there all the summer long

I hid my love in field and town
Till e'en the breeze would knock me down
The bees seemed singing ballads o'er
The fly's buzz turned a Lion's roar
And even silence found a tongue
To haunt me all the summer long
The riddle nature could not prove
Was nothing else but secret love

e. e. cummings (1894–1964)

i carry your heart with me(i carry it in

i carry your heart with me(i carry it in
my heart)i am never without it(anywhere
i go you go,my dear;and whatever is done
by only me is your doing,my darling)
                    i fear
no fate(for you are my fate,my sweet)i want
no world(for beautiful you are my world,my true)

and it's you are whatever a moon has always meant
and whatever a sun will always sing is you

here is the deepest secret nobody knows
(here is the root of the root and the bud of the bud
and the sky of the sky of a tree called life;which grows
higher than soul can hope or mind can hide)
and this is the wonder that's keeping the stars apart

i carry your heart(i carry it in my heart)

Elizabeth Barrett Browning (1806–61)

Sonnet XIV: If Thou Must Love Me ...

If thou must love me, let it be for nought
Except for love's sake only. Do not say
'I love her for her smile – her look – her way
Of speaking gently, – for a trick of thought
That falls in well with mine, and certes brought
A sense of pleasant ease on such a day' –
For these things in themselves, Beloved, may
Be changed, or change for thee, – and love, so wrought,
May be unwrought so. Neither love me for
Thine own dear pity's wiping my cheeks dry, –
A creature might forget to weep, who bore
Thy comfort long, and lose thy love thereby!
But love me for love's sake, that evermore
Thou mayst love on, through love's eternity.

Robert Browning (1812–89)

Meeting at Night

The grey sea and the long black land;
And the yellow half-moon large and low;
And the startled little waves that leap
In fiery ringlets from their sleep,
As I gain the cove with pushing prow,
And quench its speed i' the slushy sand.

Then a mile of warm sea-scented beach;
Three fields to cross till a farm appears;
A tap at the pane, the quick sharp scratch
And blue spurt of a lighted match,
And a voice less loud, thro' its joys and fears,
Than the two hearts beating each to each!

Matthew Arnold (1822–88)

The Forsaken Merman [extract]

Come, dear children, let us away;
Down and away below!
Now my brothers call from the bay,
Now the great winds shoreward blow,
Now the salt tides seaward flow;
Now the wild white horses play,
Champ and chafe and toss in the spray.
Children dear, let us away!
This way, this way!

Call her once before you go –
Call once yet!
In a voice that she will know:
'Margaret! Margaret!'
Children's voices should be dear
(Call once more) to a mother's ear;
Children's voices, wild with pain –
Surely she will come again!
Call her once and come away;
This way, this way!
'Mother dear, we cannot stay!
The wild white horses foam and fret.'
Margaret! Margaret!

Come, dear children, come away down;
Call no more!
One last look at the white-wall'd town,
And the little grey church on the windy shore;
Then come down!
She will not come though you call all day;
Come away, come away!
Children dear, was it yesterday
We heard the sweet bells over the bay?
In the caverns where we lay,
Through the surf and through the swell,
The far-off sound of a silver bell?
Sand-strewn caverns, cool and deep,
Where the winds are all asleep;
Where the spent lights quiver and gleam,
Where the salt weed sways in the stream,
Where the sea-beasts, ranged all round,
Feed in the ooze of their pasture-ground;
Where the sea-snakes coil and twine,

Dry their mail and bask in the brine;
Where great whales come sailing by,
Sail and sail, with unshut eye,
Round the world forever and aye?
When did music come this way?
Children dear, was it yesterday?

Children dear, was it yesterday
(Call yet once) that she went away?
Once she sate with you and me,
On a red gold throne in the heart of the sea,
 And the youngest sate on her knee.
She comb'd its bright hair, and she tended it well,
When down swung the sound of a far-off bell.
She sigh'd, she look'd up through the clear green sea;
She said: 'I must go, for my kinsfolk pray
In the little grey church on the shore to-day.
'Twill be Easter-time in the world – ah me!
And I lose my poor soul, Merman, here with thee.'
I said: 'Go up, dear heart, through the waves;
Say thy prayer, and come back to the kind sea-caves!'
She smil'd, she went up through the surf in the bay.
      Children dear, was it yesterday?

A. E. Housman (1859–1936)

When I Was One and Twenty

When I was one-and-twenty
I heard a wise man say,
'Give crowns and pounds and guineas
But not your heart away;
Give pearls away and rubies
But keep your fancy free.'
But I was one-and-twenty,
No use to talk to me.

When I was one-and-twenty
I heard him say again,
'The heart out of the bosom
Was never given in vain;
'Tis paid with sighs a plenty
And sold for endless rue.'
And I am two-and-twenty,
And oh, 'tis true, 'tis true.

Oscar Wilde (1854–1900)

Her Voice

The wild bee reels from bough to bough
With his furry coat and his gauzy wing,
Now in a lily-cup, and now
Setting a jacinth bell a-swing,
In his wandering;
Sit closer love: it was here I trow
I made that vow,

Swore that two lives should be like one
As long as the sea-gull loved the sea,
As long as the sunflower sought the sun, –
It shall be, I said, for eternity
'Twixt you and me!
Dear friend, those times are over and done;
Love's web is spun.

Look upward where the poplar trees
Sway and sway in the summer air,
Here in the valley never a breeze
Scatters the thistledown, but there
Great winds blow fair
From the mighty murmuring mystical seas,
And the wave-lashed leas.

Look upward where the white gull screams,
What does it see that we do not see?
Is that a star? or the lamp that gleams
On some outward voyaging argosy, –
Ah! can it be
We have lived our lives in a land of dreams!
How sad it seems.

Sweet, there is nothing left to say
But this, that love is never lost,
Keen winter stabs the breasts of May
Whose crimson roses burst his frost,
Ships tempest-tossed
Will find a harbour in some bay,
And so we may.

And there is nothing left to do
But to kiss once again, and part,

Nay, there is nothing we should rue,
I have my beauty, – you your Art,
Nay, do not start,
One world was not enough for two
Like me and you.

John Donne (1572–1631)

The Good-Morrow

I wonder, by my troth, what thou and I
Did, till we lov'd? were we not wean'd till then?
But suck'd on country pleasures, childishly?
Or snorted we in the Seven Sleepers' den?
'Twas so; but this, all pleasures fancies be.
If ever any beauty I did see,
Which I desir'd, and got, 'twas but a dream of thee.

And now good-morrow to our waking souls,
Which watch not one another out of fear;
For love, all love of other sights controls,
And makes one little room an everywhere.
Let sea-discoverers to new worlds have gone,
Let maps to others, worlds on worlds have shown;
Let us possess one world, each hath one, and is one.

My face in thine eye, thine in mine appears,
And true plain hearts do in the faces rest;
Where can we find two better hemispheres,
Without sharp North, without declining West?
Whatever dies, was not mix'd equally;
If our two loves be one, or, thou and I
Love so alike, that none do slacken, none can die.

A Valediction: Forbidding Mourning

As virtuous men pass mildly away,
And whisper to their souls to go,
Whilst some of their sad friends do say,
'The breath goes now,' and some say, 'No;'

So let us melt, and make no noise,
No tear-floods, nor sigh-tempests move,
'Twere profanation of our joys
To tell the laity our love.

Moving of th' earth brings harms and fears;
Men reckon what it did, and meant;
But trepidation of the spheres,
Though greater far, is innocent.

Dull sublunary lovers' love
(Whose soul is sense) cannot admit
Absence, because it doth remove
Those things which elemented it.

But we by a love so much refin'd,
That ourselves know not what it is,
Inter-assurèd of the mind,
Care less, eyes, lips, and hands to miss.

Our two souls therefore, which are one,
Though I must go, endure not yet
A breach, but an expansion,
Like gold to airy thinness beat.

If they be two, they are two so
As stiff twin compasses are two;
Thy soul, the fix'd foot, makes no show
To move, but doth, if th' other do.

And though it in the centre sit,
Yet when the other far doth roam,
It leans, and hearkens after it,
And grows erect, as that comes home.

Such wilt thou be to me, who must
Like th' other foot, obliquely run;
Thy firmness makes my circle just,
And makes me end, where I begun.

Katherine Mansfield (1888–1923)

Camomile Tea

Outside the sky is light with stars;
There's a hollow roaring from the sea.
And, alas! for the little almond flowers,
The wind is shaking the almond tree.

How little I thought, a year ago,
In the horrible cottage upon the Lee,
That he and I should be sitting so
And sipping a cup of camomile tea.

Light as feathers the witches fly,
The horn of the moon is plain to see;
By a firefly under a jonquil flower
A goblin toasts a bumble-bee.

We might be fifty, we might be five,
So snug, so compact, so wise are we!
Under the kitchen-table leg
My knee is pressing against his knee.

Our shutters are shut, the fire is low,
The tap is dripping peacefully;
The saucepan shadows on the wall
Are black and round and plain to see.

W. B. Yeats (1865–1939)

Aedh Wishes for the Cloths of Heaven

Had I the heavens' embroidered cloths,
Enwrought with golden and silver light,
The blue and the dim and the dark cloths
Of night and light and the half light,
I would spread the cloths under your feet:
But I, being poor, have only my dreams;
I have spread my dreams under your feet;
Tread softly because you tread on my dreams.

When You Are Old

When you are old and grey and full of sleep,
And nodding by the fire, take down this book,
And slowly read, and dream of the soft look
Your eyes had once, and of their shadows deep;

How many loved your moments of glad grace,
And loved your beauty with love false or true,
But one man loved the pilgrim soul in you,
And loved the sorrows of your changing face;

And bending down beside the glowing bars,
Murmur, a little sadly, how Love fled

And paced upon the mountains overhead
And hid his face amid a crowd of stars.

George Gordon, Lord Byron (1788–1824)

So, We'll Go No More A-Roving

So, we'll go no more a-roving
So late into the night,
Though the heart be still as loving,
And the moon be still as bright.

For the sword outwears its sheath,
And the soul wears out the breast,
And the heart must pause to breathe,
And love itself have rest.

Though the night was made for loving,
And the day returns too soon,
Yet we'll go no more a-roving
By the light of the moon.

W. H. Auden (1907–73)

O Tell Me the Truth about Love

Some say love's a little boy,
And some say it's a bird,
Some say it makes the world go around,
Some say that's absurd,
And when I asked the man next-door,

Who looked as if he knew,
His wife got very cross indeed,
And said it wouldn't do.

Does it look like a pair of pyjamas,
Or the ham in a temperance hotel?
Does its odour remind one of llamas,
Or has it a comforting smell?
Is it prickly to touch as a hedge is,
Or soft as eiderdown fluff?
Is it sharp or quite smooth at the edges?
O tell me the truth about love.

Our history books refer to it
In cryptic little notes,
It's quite a common topic on
The Transatlantic boats;
I've found the subject mentioned in
Accounts of suicides,
And even seen it scribbled on
The backs of railway guides.

Does it howl like a hungry Alsatian,
Or boom like a military band?
Could one give a first-rate imitation
On a saw or a Steinway Grand?
Is its singing at parties a riot?
Does it only like Classical stuff?
Will it stop when one wants to be quiet?
O tell me the truth about love.

I looked inside the summer-house;
It wasn't over there;
I tried the Thames at Maidenhead,

And Brighton's bracing air.
I don't know what the blackbird sang,
Or what the tulip said;
But it wasn't in the chicken-run,
Or underneath the bed.

Can it pull extraordinary faces?
Is it usually sick on a swing?
Does it spend all its time at the races,
Or fiddling with pieces of string?
Has it views of its own about money?
Does it think Patriotism enough?
Are its stories vulgar but funny?
O tell me the truth about love.

When it comes, will it come without warning
Just as I'm picking my nose?
Will it knock on my door in the morning,
Or tread in the bus on my toes?
Will it come like a change in the weather?
Will its greeting be courteous or rough?
Will it alter my life altogether?
O tell me the truth about love.

Thomas Hardy (1840–1928)

The Ruined Maid

'O 'Melia, my dear, this does everything crown!
Who could have supposed I should meet you in Town?
And whence such fair garments, such prosperi-ty?'
'O didn't you know I'd been ruined?' said she.

'You left us in tatters, without shoes or socks,
Tired of digging potatoes, and spudding up docks;
And now you've gay bracelets and bright feathers three!'
'Yes: that's how we dress when we're ruined,' said she.

'At home in the barton you said "thee" and "thou",
And "thik oon", and "theäs oon", and "t'other"; but now
Your talking quite fits 'ee for high compa-ny!'
'Some polish is gained with one's ruin,' said she.

'Your hands were like paws then, your face blue and bleak
But now I'm bewitched by your delicate cheek,
And your little gloves fit as on any la-dy!'
'We never do work when we're ruined,' said she.

'You used to call home-life a hag-ridden dream,
And you'd sigh, and you'd sock; but at present you seem
To know not of megrims or melancho-ly!'
'True. One's pretty lively when ruined,' said she.

'I wish I had feathers, a fine sweeping gown,
And a delicate face, and could strut about Town!'
'My dear – a raw country girl, such as you be,
Cannot quite expect that. You ain't ruined,' said she.

Thomas Carew (*c.* 1595–1640)

Ingrateful Beauty Threatened

Know, Celia, since thou art so proud,
'Twas I that gave thee thy renown.
Thou hadst in the forgotten crowd
Of common beauties liv'd unknown,

Had not my verse extoll'd thy name,
And with it imp'd the wings of Fame.

That killing power is none of thine;
I gave it to thy voice, and eyes;
Thy sweets, thy graces, all are mine;
Thou art my star, shin'st in my skies;
Then dart not from thy borrow'd sphere
Lightning on him that fix'd thee there.

Tempt me with such affrights no more,
Lest what I made I uncreate;
Let fools thy mystic forms adore,
I'll know thee in thy mortal state;
Wise poets, that wrapp'd Truth in tales,
Knew her themselves, through all her veils.

SIX

'Like lions to the roaring slaughter' – Battle

The earliest songs were those told of great warriors' triumphs, and it is no surprise that throughout history writers have turned to poetry to express the extremity of experience offered by war. Traditionally, and especially during the Victorian age of Empire, little boys were taught poems about bloodshed and daring deeds in the hope that they would absorb from them improving messages about bravery and patriotism. During World War I the trenches poured out verses of varying quality, as men struggled to process the horrors of battle, and many were used as propaganda – a heroic poem could be a recruitment tool, or comfort for the grieving families left behind. It was only in later years that the bitter verses of poets including Wilfred Owen – many of whom had perished in the conflict – came to be seen as the authentic voice of the fighting men.

James Elroy Flecker (1884–1915)

The Golden Journey to Samarkand [extract]

But who are ye in rags and rotten shoes,
You dirty-bearded, blocking up the way?

We are the Pilgrims, master; we shall go
Always a little further: it may be
Beyond that last blue mountain barred with snow,
Across that angry or that glimmering sea,[1]

White on a throne or guarded in a cave
There lives a prophet who can understand
Why men were born: but surely we are brave,
Who take the Golden Road to Samarkand.

…

Sweet to ride forth at evening from the wells
When shadows pass gigantic on the sand,
And softly through the silence beat the bells
Along the Golden Road to Samarkand.

We travel not for trafficking alone;
By hotter winds our fiery hearts are fanned:
For lust of knowing what should not be known
We make the Golden Journey to Samarkand.

---

1   This verse is inscribed on the memorial clock tower at the headquarters of 22 SAS Regiment
near Hereford.

Robert Southey (1774–1843)

The Battle of Blenheim

'Twas a summer evening,
Old Kaspar's work was done,
And he before his cottage door
Was sitting in the sun,
And by him sported on the green
His little grandchild Wilhelmine.

She saw her brother Peterkin
Roll something large and round
Which he beside the rivulet
In playing there had found;
He came to ask what he had found,
That was so large, and smooth, and round.

Old Kaspar took it from the boy,
Who stood expectant by;
And then the old man shook his head,
And with a natural sigh,
''Tis some poor fellow's skull,' said he,
'Who fell in the great victory.

'I find them in the garden,
For there's many here about;
And often when I go to plough,
The ploughshare turns them out!
For many thousand men,' said he,
'Were slain in that great victory.'

'Now tell us what 'twas all about,'
Young Peterkin, he cries;
And little Wilhelmine looks up

With wonder-waiting eyes;
'Now tell us all about the war,
And what they fought each other for.'

'It was the English,' Kaspar cried,
'Who put the French to rout;
But what they fought each other for
I could not well make out;
But everybody said,' quoth he,
'That 'twas a famous victory.

'My father lived at Blenheim then,
Yon little stream hard by;
They burnt his dwelling to the ground,
And he was forced to fly;
So with his wife and child he fled,
Nor had he where to rest his head.

'With fire and sword the country round
Was wasted far and wide,
And many a childing mother then,
And new-born baby died;
But things like that, you know, must be
At every famous victory.

'They said it was a shocking sight
After the field was won;
For many thousand bodies here
Lay rotting in the sun;
But things like that, you know, must be
After a famous victory.

'Great praise the Duke of Marlbro' won,
And our good Prince Eugene.'
'Why, 'twas a very wicked thing!'

Said little Wilhelmine.
'Nay . . . nay . . . my little girl,' quoth he,
'It was a famous victory.'

'And everybody praised the Duke
Who this great fight did win.'
'But what good came of it at last?'
Quoth little Peterkin.
'Why, that I cannot tell,' said he,
'But 'twas a famous victory.'

Henry Reed (1914–86)

Naming of Parts

Today we have naming of parts. Yesterday,
We had daily cleaning. And tomorrow morning,
We shall have what to do after firing. But today,
Today we have naming of parts. Japonica
Glistens like coral in all of the neighbouring gardens,
        And today we have naming of parts.

This is the lower sling swivel. And this
Is the upper sling swivel, whose use you will see,
When you are given your slings. And this is the piling swivel,
Which in your case you have not got. The branches
Hold in the gardens their silent, eloquent gestures,
        Which in our case we have not got.

This is the safety-catch, which is always released
With an easy flick of the thumb. And please do not let me
See anyone using his finger. You can do it quite easy
If you have any strength in your thumb. The blossoms

Are fragile and motionless, never letting anyone see
    Any of them using their finger.

And this you can see is the bolt. The purpose of this
Is to open the breech, as you see. We can slide it
Rapidly backwards and forwards: we call this
Easing the spring. And rapidly backwards and forwards
The early bees are assaulting and fumbling the flowers:
    They call it easing the Spring.

They call it easing the Spring: it is perfectly easy
If you have any strength in your thumb: like the bolt,
And the breech, and the cocking-piece, and the point of balance,
Which in our case we have not got; and the almond-blossom
Silent in all of the gardens and the bees going backwards and
    forwards,
    For today we have naming of parts.

Percy Bysshe Shelley (1792–1822)

The Masque of Anarchy [extract]

Stand ye calm and resolute,
Like a forest close and mute,
With folded arms and looks which are
Weapons of unvanquished war.

And if then the tyrants dare,
Let them ride among you there,
Slash, and stab, and maim and hew,
What they like, that let them do.

With folded arms and steady eyes,
And little fear, and less surprise

Look upon them as they slay
Till their rage has died away

Lord Macaulay (Thomas Babington Macaulay) (1800–59)

Horatius, from *Lays of Ancient Rome* [extract]

XXVI

But the Consul's brow was sad,
And the Consul's speech was low,
And darkly looked he at the wall,
And darkly at the foe.
'Their van will be upon us
Before the bridge goes down;
And if they once may win the bridge,
What hope to save the town?'

XXVII

Then out spake brave Horatius,
The Captain of the Gate:
'To every man upon this earth
Death cometh soon or late.
And how can man die better
Than facing fearful odds,
For the ashes of his fathers,
And the temples of his gods,

XXVIII

'And for the tender mother
Who dandled him to rest,

And for the wife who nurses
His baby at her breast,
And for the holy maidens
Who feed the eternal flame,
To save them from false Sextus
That wrought the deed of shame?

XXIX

'Haul down the bridge, Sir Consul,
With all the speed ye may;
I, with two more to help me,
Will hold the foe in play.
In yon strait path a thousand
May well be stopped by three.
Now who will stand on either hand,
And keep the bridge with me?'

XXX

Then out spake Spurius Lartius;
A Ramnian proud was he:
'Lo, I will stand at thy right hand,
And keep the bridge with thee.'
And out spake strong Herminius;
Of Titian blood was he:
'I will abide on thy left side,
And keep the bridge with thee.'

XXXI

'Horatius,' quoth the Consul,
'As thou sayest, so let it be.'
And straight against that great array
Forth went the dauntless Three.

For Romans in Rome's quarrel
Spared neither land nor gold,
Nor son nor wife, nor limb nor life,
In the brave days of old.

XXXII

Then none was for a party;
Then all were for the state;
Then the great man helped the poor,
And the poor man loved the great:
Then lands were fairly portioned;
Then spoils were fairly sold:
The Romans were like brothers
In the brave days of old.

XXXIII

Now Roman is to Roman
More hateful than a foe,
And the Tribunes beard the high,
And the Fathers grind the low.
As we wax hot in faction,
In battle we wax cold:
Wherefore men fight not as they fought
In the brave days of old.

Philip Larkin (1922–85)

MCMXIV

Those long uneven lines
Standing as patiently
As if they were stretched outside

The Oval or Villa Park,
The crowns of hats, the sun
On moustached archaic faces
Grinning as if it were all
An August Bank Holiday lark;

And the shut shops, the bleached
Established names on the sunblinds,
The farthings and sovereigns,
And dark-clothed children at play
Called after kings and queens,
The tin advertisements
For cocoa and twist, and the pubs
Wide open all day –

And the countryside not caring:
The place names all hazed over
With flowering grasses, and fields
Shadowing Domesday lines
Under wheat's restless silence;
The differently-dressed servants
With tiny rooms in huge houses,
The dust behind limousines;

Never such innocence,
Never before or since,
As changed itself to past
Without a word – the men
Leaving the gardens tidy,
The thousands of marriages,
Lasting a little while longer:
Never such innocence again.

Wilfred Owen (1893–1918)

Strange Meeting

It seemed that out of battle I escaped
Down some profound dull tunnel, long since scooped
Through granites which titanic wars had groined.

Yet also there encumbered sleepers groaned,
Too fast in thought or death to be bestirred.
Then, as I probed them, one sprang up, and stared
With piteous recognition in fixed eyes,
Lifting distressful hands, as if to bless.
And by his smile, I knew that sullen hall, –
By his dead smile I knew we stood in Hell.

With a thousand pains that vision's face was grained;
Yet no blood reached there from the upper ground,
And no guns thumped, or down the flues made moan.
'Strange friend,' I said, 'here is no cause to mourn.'
'None,' said that other, 'save the undone years,
The hopelessness. Whatever hope is yours,
Was my life also, I went hunting wild
After the wildest beauty in the world,
Which lies not calm in eyes, or braided hair,
But mocks the steady running of the hour,
And if it grieves, grieves richlier than here.
For by my glee might many men have laughed,
And of my weeping something had been left,
Which must die now. I mean the truth untold,
The pity of war, the pity war distilled.
Now men will go content with what we spoiled,
Or, discontent, boil bloody, and be spilled.
They will be swift with swiftness of the tigress.

None will break ranks, though nations trek from progress.
Courage was mine, and I had mystery,
Wisdom was mine, and I had mastery:
To miss the march of this retreating world
Into vain citadels that are not walled.
Then, when much blood had clogged their chariot-wheels,
I would go up and wash them from sweet wells,
Even with truths that lie too deep for taint.
I would have poured my spirit without stint
But not through wounds; not on the cess of war.
Foreheads of men have bled where no wounds were.

'I am the enemy you killed, my friend.
I knew you in this dark: for so you frowned
Yesterday through me as you jabbed and killed.
I parried; but my hands were loath and cold.
Let us sleep now . . . '

William Wordsworth (1770–1850)

The Prelude [extract]

The French Revolution as It Appeared to Enthusiasts at Its Commencement

Oh! pleasant exercise of hope and joy!
For mighty were the auxiliars which then stood
Upon our side, we who were strong in love!
Bliss was it in that dawn to be alive,
But to be young was very heaven!—Oh! times,
In which the meagre, stale, forbidding ways
Of custom, law, and statute, took at once

The attraction of a country in romance!
When Reason seemed the most to assert her rights,
When most intent on making of herself
A prime Enchantress – to assist the work,
Which then was going forward in her name!
Not favoured spots alone, but the whole earth,
The beauty wore of promise, that which sets
(As at some moment might not be unfelt
Among the bowers of paradise itself)
The budding rose above the rose full blown.
What temper at the prospect did not wake
To happiness unthought of? The inert
Were roused, and lively natures rapt away!
They who had fed their childhood upon dreams,
The playfellows of fancy, who had made
All powers of swiftness, subtilty, and strength
Their ministers, – who in lordly wise had stirred
Among the grandest objects of the sense,
And dealt with whatsoever they found there
As if they had within some lurking right
To wield it; – they, too, who, of gentle mood,
Had watched all gentle motions, and to these
Had fitted their own thoughts, schemers more mild,
And in the region of their peaceful selves; –
Now was it that both found, the meek and lofty
Did both find, helpers to their heart's desire,
And stuff at hand, plastic as they could wish;
Were called upon to exercise their skill,
Not in Utopia, subterranean fields,
Or some secreted island, Heaven knows where!
But in the very world, which is the world
Of all of us, – the place where in the end
We find our happiness, or not at all!

e. e. cummings (1894–1964)

next to of course god america i

'next to of course god america i
love you land of the pilgrims' and so forth oh
say can you see by the dawn's early my
country 'tis of centuries come and go
and are no more what of it we should worry
in every language even deafanddumb
thy sons acclaim your glorious name by gorry
by jingo by gee by gosh by gum
why talk of beauty what could be more beaut-
iful than these heroic happy dead
who rushed like lions to the roaring slaughter
they did not stop to think they died instead
then shall the voice of liberty be mute?'

He spoke. And drank rapidly a glass of water

Edmund Spenser (c. 1552–99)

The Faerie Queen [extract]

Canto I

The Patron of true Holinesse,
Foule Errour doth defeate:
Hypocrisie him to entrappe,
Doth to his home entreate.

A Gentle Knight was pricking on the plaine,
    Ycladd in mightie armes and silver shielde,
    Wherein old dints of deepe wounds did remaine,

The cruell markes of many a bloudy fielde;
Yet armes till that time did he never wield:
His angry steede did chide his foming bitt,
As much disdayning to the curbe to yield:
Full jolly knight he seemd, and faire did sitt,
As one for knightly giusts and fierce encounters fitt.

But on his brest a bloudie Crosse he bore,
The deare remembrance of his dying Lord,
For whose sweete sake that glorious badge he wore,
And dead as living ever him adored:
Upon his shield the like was also scored,
For soveraine hope, which in his helpe he had:
Right faithfull true he was in deede and word,
But of his cheere did seeme too solemne sad;
Yet nothing did he dread, but ever was ydrad.

Upon a great adventure he was bond,
That greatest Gloriana to him gave,
That greatest Glorious Queene of Faerie Lond,
To winne him worship, and her grace to have,
Which of all earthly things he most did crave;
And euer as he rode, his hart did earne
To prove his puissance in battell brave
Upon his foe, and his new force to learne;
Upon his foe, a Dragon horrible and stearne.

(*giusts* – jousts; *ydrad* – feared, dreaded)

Rudyard Kipling (1865–1936)

If—

If you can keep your head when all about you
Are losing theirs and blaming it on you,
If you can trust yourself when all men doubt you,
But make allowance for their doubting too;
If you can wait and not be tired by waiting,
Or being lied about, don't deal in lies,
Or being hated, don't give way to hating,
And yet don't look too good, nor talk too wise:
If you can dream – and not make dreams your master;
If you can think – and not make thoughts your aim;
If you can meet with Triumph and Disaster
And treat those two impostors just the same;
If you can bear to hear the truth you've spoken
Twisted by knaves to make a trap for fools,
Or watch the things you gave your life to, broken,
And stoop and build 'em up with worn-out tools:

If you can make one heap of all your winnings
And risk it on one turn of pitch-and-toss,
And lose, and start again at your beginnings
And never breathe a word about your loss;
If you can force your heart and nerve and sinew
To serve your turn long after they are gone,
And so hold on when there is nothing in you
Except the Will which says to them: 'Hold on!'

If you can talk with crowds and keep your virtue,
Or walk with Kings – nor lose the common touch,
if neither foes nor loving friends can hurt you,
If all men count with you, but none too much;

If you can fill the unforgiving minute
With sixty seconds' worth of distance run,
Yours is the Earth and everything that's in it,
And – which is more – you'll be a Man, my son!

G. K. Chesterton (1874–1936)

The Secret People

Smile at us, pay us, pass us; but do not quite forget;
For we are the people of England, that never have spoken yet.
There is many a fat farmer that drinks less cheerfully,
There is many a free French peasant who is richer and sadder
    than we.
There are no folk in the whole world so helpless or so wise.
There is hunger in our bellies, there is laughter in our eyes;
You laugh at us and love us, both mugs and eyes are wet:
Only you do not know us. For we have not spoken yet.

The fine French kings came over in a flutter of flags and dames.
We liked their smiles and battles, but we never could say their
    names.
The blood ran red to Bosworth and the high French lords went
    down;
There was naught but a naked people under a naked crown.
And the eyes of the King's Servants turned terribly every way,
And the gold of the King's Servants rose higher every day.
They burnt the homes of the shaven men, that had been quaint
    and kind,
Till there was no bed in a monk's house, nor food that man
    could find.

The inns of God where no man paid, that were the wall of
the weak.
The King's Servants ate them all. And still we did not speak.

And the face of the King's Servants grew greater than the King:
He tricked them, and they trapped him, and stood round him in
a ring.
The new grave lords closed round him, that had eaten the
abbey's fruits,
And the men of the new religion, with their Bibles in their boots,
We saw their shoulders moving, to menace or discuss,
And some were pure and some were vile; but none took
heed of us.
We saw the King as they killed him, and his face was proud
and pale;
And a few men talked of freedom, while England talked of ale.

A war that we understood not came over the world and woke
Americans, Frenchmen, Irish; but we knew not the things
they spoke.
They talked about rights and nature and peace and the
people's reign:
And the squires, our masters, bade us fight; and scorned us
never again.
Weak if we be for ever, could none condemn us then;
Men called us serfs and drudges; men knew that we were men.
In foam and flame at Trafalgar, on Albuera plains,
We did and died like lions, to keep ourselves in chains,
We lay in living ruins; firing and fearing not
The strange fierce face of the Frenchmen who knew for what
they fought,
And the man who seemed to be more than a man we strained
against and broke;

And we broke our own rights with him. And still we never spoke.

Our patch of glory ended; we never heard guns again.
But the squire seemed struck in the saddle; he was foolish,
    as if in pain,
He leaned on a staggering lawyer, he clutched a cringing Jew,
He was stricken; it may be, after all, he was stricken at Waterloo.
Or perhaps the shades of the shaven men, whose spoil is
    in his house,
Come back in shining shapes at last to spoil his last carouse:
We only know the last sad squires ride slowly towards the sea,
And a new people takes the land: and still it is not we.

They have given us into the hand of new unhappy lords,
Lords without anger or honour, who dare not carry their swords.
They fight by shuffling papers; they have bright dead alien eyes;
They look at our labour and laughter as a tired man looks at flies.
And the load of their loveless pity is worse than the
    ancient wrongs,
Their doors are shut in the evening; and they know no songs.

We hear men speaking for us of new laws strong and sweet,
Yet is there no man speaketh as we speak in the street.
It may be we shall rise the last as Frenchmen rose the first,
Our wrath come after Russia's wrath and our wrath be the worst.
It may be we are meant to mark with our riot and our rest
God's scorn for all men governing. It may be beer is best.
But we are the people of England; and we have not spoken yet.
Smile at us, pay us, pass us. But do not quite forget.

Elegy in a Country Churchyard

The men that worked for England
They have their graves at home:
And bees and birds of England
About the cross can roam.

But they that fought for England,
Following a falling star,
Alas, alas for England
They have their graves afar.

And they that rule in England,
In stately conclave met,
Alas, alas for England,
They have no graves as yet.

A. E. Housman (1859–1936)

Here Dead We Lie

Here dead we lie
Because we did not choose
To live and shame the land
From which we sprung.

Life, to be sure,
Is nothing much to lose,
But young men think it is,
And we were young.

SEVEN

'Far away into the silent land' – Death

Especially in earlier times, when life could indeed be nasty, brutish and short, death and the unknowable afterlife have proved fertile subjects for the imagination. No traveller can report back on this final voyage. Epitaphs like Ben Jonson's for his eldest son are deeply moving, still striking a chord with readers today because there is something universal in the subject of grief. Earlier poets viewed death in religious terms, with the comforting image of the beloved in Heaven acting as a balm for the writer and reader who have been left behind. Later, the erosion of old certainties complicated thoughts of death, and in Victorian literature a cult of beautiful, poetic morbidity emerged. Here are some of the most familiar and most evocative verses about life's final mystery.

Edgar Allen Poe (1809–40)

Annabel Lee

It was many and many a year ago,
In a kingdom by the sea,
That a maiden there lived whom you may know
By the name of Annabel Lee;
And this maiden she lived with no other thought
Than to love and be loved by me.

She was a child and *I* was a child,
In this kingdom by the sea,
But we loved with a love that was more than love –
I and my Annabel Lee –
With a love that the wingèd seraphs of Heaven
Coveted her and me.

And this was the reason that, long ago,
In this kingdom by the sea,
A wind blew out of a cloud by night,
Chilling my Annabel Lee;
So that her highborn kinsmen came
And bore her away from me,
To shut her up in a sepulchre
In this kingdom by the sea.

The angels, not half so happy in Heaven,
Went envying her and me:
Yes! that was the reason (as all men know,
In this kingdom by the sea)
That the wind came out of the cloud, chilling
And killing my Annabel Lee.

But our love it was stronger by far than the love
Of those who were older than we –
Of many far wiser than we –
And neither the angels in Heaven above,
Nor the demons down under the sea,
Can ever dissever my soul from the soul
Of the beautiful Annabel Lee.

For the moon never beams without bringing me dreams
Of the beautiful Annabel Lee;
And the stars never rise but I feel the bright eyes
Of the beautiful Annabel Lee;
And so, all the night-tide, I lie down by the side
Of my darling, my darling, my life and my bride,
In her sepulchre there by the sea –
In her tomb by the side of the sea.

John Donne (1572–1631)

Sonnet 10: Death, Be Not Proud

Death, be not proud, though some have callèd thee
Mighty and dreadful, for, thou are not so;
For those whom thou think'st, thou dost overthrow,
Die not, poor Death, nor yet canst thou kill me.
From rest and sleep, which but thy pictures be,
Much pleasure; then from thee much more must flow,
And soonest our best men with thee do go,
Rest of their bones, and soul's delivery.
Thou'art slave to fate, chance, kings, and desperate men,
And dost with poison, war, and sickness dwell,
And poppy'or charmes can make us sleep as well

And better than thy stroke; why swell'st thou then?
One short sleep past, we wake eternally,
And death shall be no more; Death, thou shalt die.

Emily Dickinson (1830–86)

Because I Could Not Stop For Death

Because I could not stop for Death –
He kindly stopped for me –
The Carriage held but just Ourselves –
And Immortality.

We slowly drove – He knew no haste
And I had put away
My labour and my leisure too,
For His Civility –

We passed the School, where Children strove
At Recess – in the Ring –
We passed the Fields of Gazing Grain –
We passed the Setting Sun –

Or rather – He passed us –
The Dews drew quivering and chill –
For only Gossamer, my Gown –
My Tippet – only Tulle –

We paused before a House that seemed
A Swelling of the Ground –
The Roof was scarcely visible –
The Cornice – in the Ground –

Since then – 'tis Centuries – and yet

Feels shorter than the Day
I first surmised the Horses' Heads
Were toward Eternity –

Elizabeth Jennings (1926–2001)

My Grandmother

She kept an antique shop – or it kept her.
Among Apostle spoons and Bristol glass,
The faded silks, the heavy furniture,
She watched her own reflection in the brass
Salvers and silver bowls, as if to prove
Polish was all, there was no need of love.

And I remember how I once refused
To go out with her, since I was afraid.
It was perhaps a wish not to be used
Like antique objects. Though she never said
That she was hurt, I still could feel the guilt
Of that refusal, guessing how she felt.

Later, too frail to keep a shop, she put
All her best things in one narrow room.
The place smelt old, of things too long kept shut,
The smell of absences where shadows come
That can't be polished. There was nothing then
To give her own reflection back again.

And when she died I felt no grief at all,
Only the guilt of what I once refused.
I walked into her room among the tall
Sideboards and cupboards – things she never used

But needed; and no finger marks were there,
Only the new dust falling through the air.

Ben Jonson (1572/3–1637)

On My First Sonne

Farewell, thou child of my right hand, and joy;
My sin was too much hope of thee, loved boy;
Seven years thou'wert lent to me, and I thee pay,
Exacted by thy fate, on the just day.
O, could I lose all father, now! for why
Will man lament the state he should envy,
To have so soon 'scaped world's and flesh's rage,
And, if no other misery, yet age?
Rest in soft peace, and, asked, say, 'Here doth lie
Ben Jonson his best piece of poetry.'
For whose sake, henceforth, all his vows be such
As what he loves may never like too much.

Alfred, Lord Tennyson (1809–92)

Mariana

With blackest moss the flower-plots
Were thickly crusted, one and all:
The rusted nails fell from the knots
That held the pear to the gable-wall.
The broken sheds looked sad and strange:
Unlifted was the clinking latch;
Weeded and worn the ancient thatch

Upon the lonely moated grange.
She only said, 'My life is dreary,
He cometh not,' she said;
She said, 'I am aweary, aweary,
I would that I were dead!'

Her tears fell with the dews at even;
Her tears fell ere the dews were dried;
She could not look on the sweet heaven,
Either at morn or eventide.
After the flitting of the bats,
When thickest dark did trance the sky,
She drew her casement-curtain by,
And glanced athwart the glooming flats.
She only said, 'My life is dreary,
He cometh not,' she said;
She said, 'I am aweary, aweary,
I would that I were dead!'

Upon the middle of the night,
Waking she heard the night-fowl crow:
The cock sung out an hour ere light:
From the dark fen the oxen's low
Came to her: without hope of change,
In sleep she seemed to walk forlorn,
Till cold winds woke the grey-eyed morn
About the lonely moated grange.
She only said, 'The day is dreary,
He cometh not,' she said;
She said, 'I am aweary, aweary,
I would that I were dead!'

About a stone-cast from the wall
A sluice with blackened waters slept,

And o'er it many, round and small,
The clustered marish-mosses crept.
Hard by a poplar shook alway,
All silver-green with gnarlèd bark:
For leagues no other tree did mark
The level waste, the rounding grey.
She only said, 'My life is dreary,
He cometh not,' she said;
She said, 'I am aweary, aweary,
I would that I were dead!'

And ever when the moon was low,
And the shrill winds were up and away
In the white curtain, to and fro,
She saw the gusty shadow sway.
But when the moon was very low,
And wild winds bound within their cell,
The shadow of the poplar fell
Upon her bed, across her brow.
She only said, 'The night is dreary,
He cometh not,' she said;
She said, 'I am aweary, aweary,
I would that I were dead!'

All day within the dreamy house,
The doors upon their hinges creaked;
The blue fly sung in the pane; the mouse
Behind the mouldering wainscot shrieked,
Or from the crevice peered about.
Old faces glimmered through the doors,
Old footsteps trod the upper floors,
Old voices called her from without.
She only said, 'My life is dreary,
He cometh not,' she said;

She said, 'I am aweary, aweary,
I would that I were dead!'

The sparrow's chirrup on the roof,
The slow clock ticking, and the sound
Which to the wooing wind aloof
The poplar made, did all confound
Her sense; but most she loathed the hour
When the thick-moted sunbeam lay
Athwart the chambers, and the day
Was sloping toward his western bower.
Then, said she, 'I am very dreary,
He will not come,' she said;
She wept, 'I am aweary, aweary,
O God, that I were dead!'

William Collins (1721–59)

How Sleep the Brave

How sleep the brave, who sink to rest
By all their country's wishes blest!
When Spring, with dewy fingers cold,
Returns to deck their hallowed mould,
She there shall dress a sweeter sod
Than Fancy's feet have ever trod.

By fairy hands their knell is rung,
By forms unseen their dirge is sung;
There Honour comes, a pilgrim grey,
To bless the turf that wraps their clay;
And Freedom shall awhile repair,
To dwell a weeping hermit there!

Christina Rossetti (1830–94)

Remember Me

Remember me when I am gone away,
Gone far away into the silent land;
When you can no more hold me by the hand,
Nor I half turn to go, yet turning stay.
Remember me when no more day by day
You tell me of our future that you planned:
Only remember me; you understand
It will be late to counsel then or pray.
Yet if you should forget me for a while
And afterwards remember, do not grieve:
For if the darkness and corruption leave
A vestige of the thoughts that once I had,
Better by far you should forget and smile
Than that you should remember and be sad.

Algernon Charles Swinburne (1837–1909)

The Garden of Proserpine [extract]

Here, where the world is quiet,
Here, where all trouble seems
Dead winds' and spent waves' riot
In doubtful dreams of dreams;
I watch the green field growing
For reaping folk and sowing,
For harvest-time and mowing,
A sleepy world of streams.

I am tired of tears and laughter,
And men that laugh and weep;
Of what may come hereafter
For men that sow to reap:
I am weary of days and hours,
Blown buds of barren flowers,
Desires and dreams and powers
And everything but sleep.

. . .

Pale, without name or number,
In fruitless fields of corn,
They bow themselves and slumber
All night till light is born;
And like a soul belated,
In hell and heaven unmated,
By cloud and mist abated
Comes out of darkness morn.

. . .

Pale, beyond porch and portal,
Crowned with calm leaves, she stands
Who gathers all things mortal
With cold immortal hands;
Her languid lips are sweeter
Than love's who fears to greet her
To men that mix and meet her
From many times and lands.

. . .

We are not sure of sorrow,
And joy was never sure;

Today will die tomorrow;
Time stoops to no man's lure;
And love, grown faint and fretful,
With lips but half regretful
Sighs, and with eyes forgetful
Weeps that no loves endure.

From too much love of living,
From hope and fear set free,
We thank with brief thanksgiving
Whatever gods may be
That no life lives for ever;
That dead men rise up never;
That even the weariest river
Winds somewhere safe to sea.

Then star nor sun shall waken,
Nor any change of light:
Nor sound of waters shaken,
Nor any sound or sight:
Nor wintry leaves nor vernal,
Nor days nor things diurnal;
Only the sleep eternal
In an eternal night.

Thomas Moore (1779–1852)

The Last Rose of Summer

'Tis the last rose of summer
Left blooming alone;
All her lovely companions
Are faded and gone;

No flower of her kindred,
No rosebud is nigh,
To reflect back her blushes,
To give sigh for sigh.

I'll not leave thee, thou lone one!
To pine on the stem;
Since the lovely are sleeping,
Go, sleep thou with them.
Thus kindly I scatter
Thy leaves o'er the bed,
Where thy mates of the garden
Lie scentless and dead.

So soon may I follow,
When friendships decay,
And from Love's shining circle
The gems drop away.
When true hearts lie withered
And fond ones are flown,
Oh! who would inhabit
This bleak world alone?

W. H. Auden (1907–73)

Musée des Beaux Arts

About suffering they were never wrong,
The Old Masters: how well they understood
Its human position: how it takes place
While someone else is eating or opening a window or just
    walking dully along;
How, when the aged are reverently, passionately waiting

For the miraculous birth, there always must be
Children who did not specially want it to happen, skating
On a pond at the edge of the wood:
They never forgot
That even the dreadful martyrdom must run its course
Anyhow in a corner, some untidy spot
Where the dogs go on with their doggy life and the torturer's
    horse
Scratches its innocent behind on a tree.

In Breughel's *Icarus*, for instance: how everything turns away
Quite leisurely from the disaster; the ploughman may
Have heard the splash, the forsaken cry,
But for him it was not an important failure; the sun shone
As it had to on the white legs disappearing into the green
Water; and the expensive delicate ship that must have seen
Something amazing, a boy falling out of the sky,
Had somewhere to get to and sailed calmly on.

Alan Seeger (1888–1916)

I Have a Rendezvous with Death

I have a rendezvous with Death
At some disputed barricade,
When Spring comes back with rustling shade
And apple-blossoms fill the air –
I have a rendezvous with Death
When Spring brings back blue days and fair.

It may be he shall take my hand
And lead me into his dark land
And close my eyes and quench my breath –

It may be I shall pass him still.
I have a rendezvous with Death
On some scarred slope of battered hill,
When Spring comes round again this year
And the first meadow-flowers appear.

God knows 'twere better to be deep
Pillowed in silk and scented down,
Where love throbs out in blissful sleep,
Pulse nigh to pulse, and breath to breath,
Where hushed awakenings are dear . . .
But I've a rendezvous with Death
At midnight in some flaming town,
When Spring trips north again this year,
And I to my pledged word am true,
I shall not fail that rendezvous.

EIGHT

'Wonderful deathless ditties'
– A Ragbag

These are all the verses that were simply impossible to categorize, gathered here because it seemed such a shame to exclude them altogether. They stand as proof that poetry can deal with any subject and tell any story – from that of the grandson of the Mongol emperor Genghis Khan, to that of a fictional ratcatcher.

Arthur O'Shaughnessy (1844–81)

Ode

We are the music-makers,
And we are the dreamers of dreams,
Wandering by lone sea-breakers,
And sitting by desolate streams;
World-losers and world-forsakers,
On whom the pale moon gleams:
Yet we are the movers and shakers
Of the world for ever, it seems.

With wonderful deathless ditties
We build up the world's great cities,
And out of a fabulous story
We fashion an empire's glory:
One man with a dream, at pleasure,
Shall go forth and conquer a crown;
And three with a new song's measure
Can trample an empire down.

We, in the ages lying
In the buried past of the earth,
Built Nineveh with our sighing,
And Babel itself with our mirth;
And o'erthrew them with prophesying
To the old of the new world's worth;
For each age is a dream that is dying,
Or one that is coming to birth.

Ezra Pound (1885–1972)

Song in the Manner of Housman

O woe, woe,
People are born and die,
We also shall be dead pretty soon
Therefore let us act as if we were dead already.

The bird sits on the hawthorn tree
But he dies also, presently.
Some lads get hung, and some get shot.
Woeful is this human lot.
Woe! woe, etcetera ...

London is a woeful place,
Shropshire is much pleasanter.
Then let us smile a little space
Upon fond nature's morbid grace.
Oh, Woe, woe, woe, etcetera ...

John Betjeman (1906–84)

How to Get On in Society

Phone for the fish knives, Norman
As cook is a little unnerved;
You kiddies have crumpled the serviettes
And I must have things daintily served.

Are the requisites all in the toilet?
The frills round the cutlets can wait
Till the girl has replenished the cruets
And switched on the logs in the grate.

It's ever so close in the lounge dear,
But the vestibule's comfy for tea
And Howard is riding on horseback
So do come and take some with me.

Now here is a fork for your pastries
And do use the couch for your feet;
I know that I wanted to ask you –
Is trifle sufficient for sweet?

Milk and then just as it comes dear?
I'm afraid the preserve's full of stones;
Beg pardon, I'm soiling the doileys
With afternoon tea-cakes and scones.

Fleur Adcock (1934–)

The Soho Hospital for Women [extract]

Nellie has only one breast
ample enough to make several.
Her quilted dressing-gown softens
to semi-doubtful this imbalance
and there's no starched vanity
in our abundant ward-mother:
her silvery hair's in braids, her slippers
loll, her weathered smile holds true.
When she dresses up in her black
with her glittering marcasite brooch on
to go for the weekly radium treatment
she's the bright star of the taxi-party –
whatever may be growing under her ribs.

*

Doris hardly smokes in the ward –
and hardly eats more than a dreamy spoonful –
but the corridors and bathrooms
reek of her Players Number 10,
and the drug-trolley pauses
for long minutes by her bed.
Each week for the taxi-outing
she puts on her skirt again
and has to pin the slack waistband
more tightly over her scarlet sweater.
Her face, a white shadow through smoked glass,
lets Soho display itself unregarded.

*

Third in the car is Mrs Golding
who never smiles. And why should she?

Horace (Quintus Horatius Flaccus, 65 BC–8 BC)

Happy the Man

Happy the man, and happy he alone,
he who can call today his own:
he who, secure within, can say,
Tomorrow do thy worst, for I have lived today.

Be fair or foul, or rain or shine
the joys I have possessed, in spite of fate, are mine.
Not Heaven itself, upon the past has power,
but what has been, has been, and I have had my hour.

Samuel Taylor Coleridge (1772–1834)

Kubla Khan
Or, a Vision in a Dream. A Fragment.

In Xanadu did Kubla Khan
A stately pleasure-dome decree:
Where Alph, the sacred river, ran
Through caverns measureless to man
    Down to a sunless sea.
So twice five miles of fertile ground
With walls and towers were girdled round:
And there were gardens bright with sinuous rills,
Where blossomed many an incense-bearing tree;
And here were forests ancient as the hills,
Enfolding sunny spots of greenery.
But oh! that deep romantic chasm which slanted
Down the green hill athwart a cedarn cover!
A savage place! as holy and enchanted
As e'er beneath a waning moon was haunted
By woman wailing for her demon-lover!
And from this chasm, with ceaseless turmoil seething,
As if this earth in fast thick pants were breathing,
A mighty fountain momently was forced:
Amid whose swift half-intermitted burst
Huge fragments vaulted like rebounding hail,
Or chaffy grain beneath the thresher's flail:
And 'mid these dancing rocks at once and ever
It flung up momently the sacred river.

Five miles meandering with a mazy motion
Through wood and dale the sacred river ran,
Then reached the caverns measureless to man,
And sank in tumult to a lifeless ocean:
And 'mid this tumult Kubla heard from far
Ancestral voices prophesying war!
The shadow of the dome of pleasure
    Floated midway on the waves;
    Where was heard the mingled measure
    From the fountain and the caves.
    It was a miracle of rare device,
    A sunny pleasure-dome with caves of ice!

    A damsel with a dulcimer
    In a vision once I saw:
    It was an Abyssinian maid,
    And on her dulcimer she played,
    Singing of Mount Abora.
    Could I revive within me
    Her symphony and song,
    To such a deep delight 'twould win me,
That with music loud and long,
I would build that dome in air,
That sunny dome! those caves of ice!
And all who heard should see them there,
And all should cry, Beware! Beware!
His flashing eyes, his floating hair!
Weave a circle round him thrice,
And close your eyes with holy dread,
For he on honey-dew hath fed,
And drunk the milk of Paradise.

The Pains of Sleep

Ere on my bed my limbs I lay,
It hath not been my use to pray
With moving lips or bended knees;
But silently, by slow degrees,
My spirit I to Love compose,
In humble trust mine eyelids close,
With reverential resignation,
No wish conceived, no thought expressed,
Only a sense of supplication;
A sense o'er all my soul impressed
That I am weak, yet not unblessed,
Since in me, round me, every where
Eternal strength and wisdom are.

But yester-night I prayed aloud
In anguish and in agony,
Up-starting from the fiendish crowd
Of shapes and thoughts that tortured me:
A lurid light, a trampling throng,
Sense of intolerable wrong,
And whom I scorned, those only strong!
Thirst of revenge, the powerless will
Still baffled, and yet burning still!
Desire with loathing strangely mixed
On wild or hateful objects fixed.
Fantastic passions! maddening brawl!
And shame and terror over all!
Deeds to be hid which were not hid,
Which all confused I could not know
Whether I suffered, or I did:
For all seemed guilt, remorse or woe,

My own or others still the same
Life-stifling fear, soul-stifling shame.

So two nights passed: the night's dismay
Saddened and stunned the coming day.
Sleep, the wide blessing, seemed to me
Distemper's worst calamity.
The third night, when my own loud scream
Had waked me from the fiendish dream,
O'ercome with sufferings strange and wild,
I wept as I had been a child;
And having thus by tears subdued
My anguish to a milder mood,
Such punishments, I said, were due
To natures deepliest stained with sin, –
For aye entempesting anew
The unfathomable hell within,
The horror of their deeds to view,
To know and loathe, yet wish and do!
Such griefs with such men well agree,
But wherefore, wherefore fall on me?
To be loved is all I need,
And whom I love, I love indeed.

George Gordon, Lord Byron (1788–1824)

Epitaph to a Dog

Near this spot
Are deposited the Remains
Of one
Who possessed Beauty
Without Vanity,
Strength without Insolence,
Courage without Ferocity,
And all the Virtues of Man
Without his Vices.

The Price, which would be unmeaning flattery
If inscribed over Human Ashes,
Is but a just tribute to the Memory of
'Boatswain,' a Dog
Who was born at Newfoundland,
May, 1803,
And died in Newstead Abbey,
Nov. 18, 1808.

When some proud son of man returns to earth,
Unknown by glory, but upheld by birth,
The sculptor's art exhausts the pomp of woe,
And storied urns record who rests below.
When all is done, upon the tomb is seen
Not what he was, but what he should have been.
But the poor dog, in life the firmest friend,
The first to welcome, foremost to defend,
Whose honest heart is still his master's own,
Who labours, fights, lives, breathes for him alone,

Unhonoured falls, unnoticed all his worth,
Denied in heaven the soul he held on earth –
While man, vain insect! hopes to be forgiven,
And claims himself a sole exclusive heaven.

Oh man! thou feeble tenant of an hour,
Debased by slavery, or corrupt by power –
Who knows thee well must quit thee with disgust,
Degraded mass of animated dust!
Thy love is lust, thy friendship all a cheat,
Thy smiles hypocrisy, thy words deceit!
By nature vile, ennobled but by name,
Each kindred brute might bid thee blush for shame.
Ye, who behold perchance this simple urn,
Pass on, it honours none you wish to mourn.
To mark a friend's remains these stones arise;
I never knew but one – and here he lies.

Robert Browning (1812–89)

The Pied Piper of Hamelin [extract]

Into the street the Piper stepped,
Smiling first a little smile,
As if he knew what magic slept
In his quiet pipe the while;
Then, like a musical adept,
To blow the pipe his lips he wrinkled,
And green and blue his sharp eyes twinkled
Like a candle flame where salt is sprinkled;
And ere three shrill notes the pipe uttered,
You heard as if an army muttered;

And the muttering grew to a grumbling;
And the grumbling grew to a mighty rumbling;
And out of the houses the rats came tumbling:
Great rats, small rats, lean rats, brawny rats,
Brown rats, black rats, grey rats, tawny rats,
Grave old plodders, gay young friskers,
Fathers, mothers, uncles, cousins,
Cocking tails and pricking whiskers,
Families by tens and dozens,
Brothers, sisters, husbands, wives –
Followed the Piper for their lives.
From street to street he piped advancing,
And step for step they followed dancing,
Until they came to the river Weser,
Wherein all plunged and perished!

Notes on the Poets and Poems

Fleur Adcock (1934–) The Soho Hospital for Women [extract]

Adcock moved from her native New Zealand to England during the war years with her parents, who dug ditches for the war effort, and she eventually settled in London in 1963. She has been married twice to men of letters – her fellow poet Alistair Campbell and author Barry Crump – and she is a shrewd observer of relationships in her work.

Allan Ahlberg (1938–) Scissors

Ahlberg spent a decade as a primary-school teacher, and it certainly shows in his two sharply observed poetry collections *Please Mrs Butler* and *Heard It In The Playground*. He has produced over a hundred books for children of all ages, often working closely with his late wife Janet, who provided the witty illustrations.

Anonymous Sumer Is Icumen In / Sir Patrick Spens

'Sumer is icumen in' is a traditional English round known only from a manuscript from Reading Abbey, estimated to date from around 1260. It has the distinction of being the earliest-known round, the earliest piece of six-part polyphonic music, and the earliest example of a piece of music with both secular and religious lyrics. The religious lyrics are in Latin and concern the Crucifixion; the better-known Middle English secular words, in Wessex dialect, celebrate the arrival of summer.

Although Scots, 'Sir Patrick Spens' was one of the works collected in Thomas Percy's *Reliques of Ancient English Poetry* (1765) and later included by F. J. Child in his *The English and Scottish Popular Ballads* (1882–98). No date is given for its composition and there are many different versions, but the story this ancient ballad tells is essentially the same. It seems to be an amalgam of two accounts of actual voyages undertaken by thirteenth-century Scots noblemen sent to escort royal princesses (there is, however, no historical record of a Sir Patrick Spens or Spence). The version here is close to that in Percy's *Reliques*.

Matthew Arnold (1822–88) The Forsaken Merman [extract]

Arnold's father Thomas was a famous headmaster at Rugby public school, so he must have been rather horrified by his son's foppish, rebellious behaviour at Oxford University. However, Matthew eventually achieved renown and respect as a critic, and submitted to a responsible day job as a committed schools inspector to win the hand of Frances Whiteman, whose father wisely refused to let her marry a man with no prospects. Most of his poetry was written in his twenties and thirties: he said that after his thirtieth birthday he felt 'three parts iced over'.

W. H. Auden (1907–73) Tell Me The Truth About Love / Musée des Beaux Arts

Auden's early poems had a Romantic flavour, though he later scornfully rejected the poets he referred to as 'Kelly and Sheets' and turned towards modernism. He was politically active, and greatly affected by his experiences fighting on the Republican side in the Spanish Civil War in 1937. Though homosexual, Auden married Erika, the daughter of the German writer Thomas Mann, to enable her to flee Nazi persecution. He moved to the United States, eventually taking American citizenship in 1946, and began a relationship with writer Chester Kallman. They wrote operas together.

Hilaire Belloc (1870–1953) Jim

Generations of parents have cheerfully scared the living daylights out of their children with Belloc's *Cautionary Tales* (1907). Matilda told lies and was burnt to death, but the unfortunate Henry King, whom Belloc tells us was 'early cut off in Dreadful agonies', committed no graver sin than chewing pieces of string. A staunch Catholic and prolific writer in many genres, Belloc was drafted in to produce propaganda during World War I and confided in his closest friend, **G. K. Chesterton**, that 'it is sometimes necessary to lie damnably in the interests of the nation' – and, presumably, the interests of disobedient, string-munching youngsters.

John Betjeman (1906–84) Diary of a Church Mouse / How to Get On in Society

Betjeman's witty verses were undervalued as lightweight throughout the 1950s and 1960s, though they are now some of England's most cherished for their air of gentle nostalgia. His love for the provincial landscape (excepting, of course, Slough) – and affectionate lampoons of its familiar characters – was informed by his work on the Shell motoring guides to English counties. He partied hard while studying at Oxford, frequently with his teddy bear Archibald Ormsby-Gore in tow, a detail that inspired Evelyn Waugh when he came to create Sebastian Flyte of *Brideshead Revisited* and his bear, Aloysius.

Notes on the Poets and Poems

William Blake (1757–1827) The Tyger / Auguries of Innocence

Blake was a true radical and visionary who frequently saw angels, and contemporary accounts describe his blazing eyes and wild hair. He illustrated his poems himself and printed them by hand, but did not achieve any kind of fame until late in his life. Long after his death, Blake was rediscovered by the Pre-Raphaelites and, later, Ginsberg and the Beat poets, and he came to be seen as the original Romantic genius, writing and painting with passionate originality. He married Caroline Boucher, the beautiful daughter of a market gardener, and taught her to read so that she could assist him in his work. Their lessons occasionally startled the neighbours – one account describes them reading *Paradise Lost* together in the summerhouse, stark naked.

Emily Brontë (1818–48) No Coward Soul Is Mine

Emily grew up with her sisters Charlotte and Anne, her dissolute brother Branwell, and her father the rector at Haworth, on the Yorkshire Moors. With her youngest sister Anne she created the imaginary realm of Gondal, and much of her poetry was written about its history and mythology. In 1846 the sisters, under the pseudonyms of Currer, Ellis and Acton Bell, published a volume of poems that sold only two copies in a year. We must be thankful for the lack of public enthusiasm, because the disappointment inspired them to turn to fiction. Charlotte produced her masterpiece *Jane Eyre*, and Emily the extraordinary *Wuthering Heights*. Anne (who was rather unfortunate to have such talented sisters) published *The Tenant of Wildfell Hall*. Emily nursed Branwell through his final illness, caught a cold at the funeral and died, still tragically young, of consumption.

Elizabeth Barrett Browning (1806–61) If Thou Must Love Me . . .

Well-educated at home by her loving but over-protective father, Elizabeth began writing young. Her beloved brother Edward drowned while they visited Torquay to improve Elizabeth's health and she became an invalid, withdrawing from the world, on her return to London. Her poems were madly popular, though, and won her admiration from eminent figures including **Tennyson**, Dante Gabriel Rossetti, John Ruskin and a young poet six years her junior: **Robert Browning**. They defied her father – who never forgave Elizabeth – by marrying, and moved to Italy where their son was born. She died in Robert's arms in Florence.

Robert Browning (1812–89) Meeting At Night / The Pied Piper of Hamelin [extract]

Browning was a precocious child who received much of his education from home tutors, which explains why many of his poems feature pretty obscure references: he wrongly assumed that his readers would have the same breadth of learning that he did. In 1845 he met and fell passionately in love with the poet **Elizabeth Barrett Browning**, then an invalid living a reclusive life. They eloped against her overbearing father's wishes and lived happily in Italy with their adored son, nicknamed Pen, until her death in 1861. She was by far the more celebrated poet during her lifetime, though Robert has since taken his place as one of the greats of Victorian literature.

Robert Burns (1759–96) To a Mouse

Burns was a farmer's son, a good-looking charmer who managed to father a number of illegitimate children, including two sets of twins with the long-suffering Jean Armour, whom he later married. His best work was written in the Scots dialect – the Romantics later hero-worshipped him for writing in the natural voice of his people – and he collected Scottish folk songs, including some racy ones which he enjoyed circulating in private to his friends.

George Gordon, Lord Byron (1788–1824) So We'll Go No More A-Roving / Epitaph to a Dog

Byron boasted an ancestry of wild and eccentric aristocrats who had frittered away the wealth of the estate he inherited aged ten. Born with a club foot and a caul – a membrane covering his face, which was seen as an ill omen – he was an unlikely heart-throb, especially since he was perpetually dieting due to a tendency to chubbiness. The ladies were undeterred and his many lovers included an auburn-haired maid in his childhood, crazy Caroline Lamb who had herself delivered to him naked on a silver platter, Teresa Guiccioli, who was married to an aged Italian count but lived with Byron in Venice, and his own half-sister Augusta Leigh, whose daughter he possibly fathered. His marriage was, unsurprisingly, not a success. He fought for the Greeks – to whom he is still a national hero – against the Turks and proved a surprisingly good general; his heart is buried in Greece.

Byron's 'Epitaph to a Dog' was written in memory of his beloved Newfoundland, Boatswain, whose memorial at Newstead Abbey is larger than the poet's.

Thomas Carew (*c.* 1595–1640) Ingrateful Beauty Threatened

Carew (pronounced Carey, confusingly) was one of the most dazzling and decadent of the Cavalier poets at the court of King Charles I. He eventually rose to become a server to the king. Allegedly, he owed his preferment to the queen because, when lighting the king to bed one night, he had happened upon her behaving rather friskily with Lord St Albans, and dropped the candle to spare her blushes. Much of his poetry is addressed to a mysterious, and clearly capricious, Celia. Although his verses circulated at court during his lifetime, by the time they were posthumously published they had a chiefly nostalgic appeal for the Royalists.

Lewis Carroll (1832–98) You Are Old, Father William / The Walrus and the Carpenter

Charles Lutwidge Dodgson was a stammering professor of mathematics at Oxford who found himself most at home in the company of children, to whom he recounted his fantastic tales. His pseudonym Lewis Carroll was created by translating his first and middle names into Latin, reversing the order of them, and translating them back into English, a typically scholarly piece of word play. It can't be denied that the Alice stories have a strange inverted logic to them and perhaps it is this that has enabled them to be read in all sorts of serious and satirical ways. Carroll gave his illustrator John Tenniel three choices of second character in 'The Walrus and the Carpenter': Tenniel was to choose between a carpenter, a butterfly or a baronet as each one would scan equally well. It's hard to see how a butterfly would have looked tucking in to this peculiar picnic on the beach, though.

John Clare (1793–1864) Song

Clare was from an almost illiterate farming family and composed poems while toiling in the fields. A canny publisher hyped him as the 'Northamptonshire peasant poet' and he was petted and praised by literary London for his rustic rhymes. He refused to allow his punctuation to be 'corrected', and he relished the high life, but fashion proved fickle and his later poems flopped. Unable to return to the fields – the other labourers worried that he might write unflattering verses about them – Clare sank into madness. He was institutionalized but continued writing. In the asylum he believed that he was married to his first love, Mary Joyce, which must have riled his wife and the mother of his seven children, Patty Turner. As he also claimed to be both **Shakespeare** and **Byron**, perhaps she turned a blind eye.

G. K. Chesterton (1874–1936) The Secret People / Elegy in a Country Churchyard

Chesterton is also known as the author of the Father Brown mystery stories, and the surreal, anarchic conspiracy thriller *The Man Who Was Thursday*. An anti-Establishment thread runs through all his work: his writing, including his journalism and biographies, gives the underdog a voice while celebrating the idea of Englishness. He was also influenced by his conversion to Catholicism, perhaps at the prompting of his closest friend, fellow poet **Hilaire Belloc**. They were so close that George Bernard Shaw coined the word 'Chesterbelloc' to describe them. In his 'Elegy in a Country Churchyard', Chesterton uses the title of Thomas Grey's eighteenth-century masterpiece to attack the politicians who sent so many young men to their senseless deaths during World War I.

Samuel Taylor Coleridge (1772–1834) Kubla Khan / The Pains of Sleep

Coleridge was brilliant but troubled and, throughout his life, embarked on numerous projects that came to nothing. His plan to found a commune with **Southey** failed, he was an abysmal soldier during a brief spell in the Royal Dragoons, his marriage to Sara Fricker was unhappy – partly because he later fell in love with **Wordsworth**'s sister-in-law – and he was unable to shake the addiction to laudanum that probably inspired 'Kubla Khan'. However, his contribution to Romanticism from its earliest days is now recognized, and his collaboration with Wordsworth on *Lyrical Ballads* (1798) is often taken as the starting date of the movement.

William Collins (1721–59) How Sleep The Brave

After leaving Oxford University, Collins was unsure about his path: he didn't manage to win a fellowship, wasn't drawn to the Church and, according to a rather unsupportive uncle, was too lazy to join the armed forces. He moved to London, where he fell in with a literary crowd including Dr Johnson, and embarked on a writing career. His passionate poems did not adhere to the era's taste for restrained, elegant verse, though they did prove hugely influential after his death: his wildness and imagination made him a hero of the Romantics. Poor Collins could not have foreseen this, however, and a combination of disappointment and the demon drink drove him mad.

Abraham Cowley (1618–67) Drinking

The precocious Cowley had read **Spenser**'s *Faerie Queen* twice before he went to school, where he produced a poem about Pyramus and Thisbe aged only ten, and achieved fame in his teens. The Civil War interrupted his university education, and he became a confidant of the exiled Queen, Henrietta Maria, passing coded letters from her to her husband, Charles I. Although he turned his hand to some rather erotic verses, it was claimed that he was in fact painfully shy around women, and diverted himself with varied interests including science and botany, instead of love. Presumably, he was also fond of a tipple.

e. e. cummings (1894–1964) i carry your heart with me / 'next to of course god america i

It isn't clear exactly why e. e. cummings generally appears in lower case: the poet sometimes signed himself thus, and he was famously experimental with typography, but his widow claimed that he had never legally changed his name. His first book described his wrongful arrest and incarceration in a French prison in 1917. It brought him fame, and he followed it up with poetry, essays, plays and, oddly, a never-performed satirical ballet based on *Uncle Tom's Cabin*. cummings's diverse influences included **Swinburne**, jazz and Dadaism and he was gleefully experimental with form, although he could also turn out a fine traditional sonnet when he fancied it. He was a firm believer in UFOs.

W. H. Davies (1871–1940) The Kingfisher

It is a little surprising that William Henry Davies was championed by literary figures including George Bernard Shaw and Edward Thomas, given that he accurately entitled his memoirs *The Autobiography of a Super-Tramp*. Raised by his grandparents in Wales, he left school in his teens and ended up on the road in America, losing a leg train-hopping in Canada. His ramshackle lifestyle – a day's begging or casual work was usually followed by drinking the proceeds – did not diminish the popularity of his poems. Settling down did not render him any less disreputable, since he eventually married a pregnant prostitute half his age whom he had met at a bus stop.

Emily Dickinson (1830–86) Because I Could Not Stop For Death

Dickinson's family were prominent citizens of Amherst, Massachusetts, but in her twenties she withdrew almost entirely from the world, took to dressing in white and wrote nearly two thousand of her deceptively simple, melancholy poems. It was perhaps a failed romance that led her to shut herself away: love letters addressed to a mysterious 'Master' were discovered among her papers, poems and recipes (she was a keen and fastidious cook). Only a handful of her verses were published before her death and, until 1955, her eccentric punctuation was 'corrected' – it was only in the late twentieth century that her originality was at last appreciated.

John Donne (1572–1631) The Good-Morrow / A Valediction: Forbidding Mourning / Sonnet 10: Death, Be Not Proud

Sex and religion preoccupy Donne as much in his verse as they did during his life. Following a dissolute youth, he married his beloved wife Anne in defiance of her father and they went on to produce twelve children. All the more unusual, then, that he never remarried after her death, because presumably an extra pair of hands would have come in useful. Donne was from Catholic stock at a time when this was a hindrance in public life and could even prove dangerous, and King James VI and I – sensing that his passion and wit would render him a superstar Anglican preacher – persuaded him into the Church of England. From its pulpits – notably that of St Paul's Cathedral, where he was the Dean – he delivered the high-flown sermons that include some of his best-known lines, including 'No man is an Island'. Often preoccupied with death, Donne even posed in a shroud for his own memorial.

Max Ehrmann (1872–1945) Desiderata

Ehrmann was an Indiana lawyer whose poems received little attention during his lifetime, although his widow published his work after his death. In 1959, the vicar at St Paul's Church in Baltimore included 'Desiderata' – the Latin title means 'things that are desired' – in a pamphlet for his congregation. The church's headed paper included its foundation date of 1692 and, somehow, the myth sprung up that this was when the verses had been composed. Later vicars rather rued the error: one complained in the 1970s about the troublesome volume of queries he received about the poem. 'Desiderata' was enthusiastically embraced by the San Francisco hippy movement, and was reproduced on posters that adorned many a bedsit wall.

T. S. Eliot (1888-1965) The Song of the Jellicles / The Journey of the Magi

Eliot's innovative, modernist verse revolutionized poetry when he published *The Waste Land* in 1922. His unstable first wife Vivien assisted in its writing, but the relationship soured – after their separation she took to wearing a placard reading 'I am the wife he abandoned' to his lectures. Eliot later married Valerie, his secretary at the publisher Faber & Faber where he nurtured up-and-coming poetic talent. His many-layered work often consists of a tapestry of allusions, references, quotations and, sometimes, private jokes.

Ezra Pound christened Eliot 'Old Possum', and the latter put this name to *Old Possum's Book of Practical Cats*, a collection of feline-themed poems originally written in letters to his godchildren. The best-known adaptation of the verses is the Andrew Lloyd Webber musical *Cats*.

James Elroy Flecker (1884–1915) The Golden Journey to Samarkand [extract]

Flecker's first name was originally Herman. He studied at both Oxford and Cambridge where he cut quite a dash, professing agnosticism and embracing the Aesthetic Movement, which admired art for art's sake. He wrote plays and a rather tricky experimental novel, but showed most promise as a poet. He was inspired by his travels in the East with the consular service, but he died of tuberculosis aged only thirty with his finest work perhaps still unwritten.

Robert Graves (1895–1985) In the Wilderness

Graves enlisted for World War I in 1914 straight from school, and his autobiography *Goodbye to All That* relates how he read the inaccurate news of his own demise in *The Times*. His first marriage combusted when the domineering American poet (and man-eater) Laura Riding arrived like a whirlwind in London. He fled society and his family to live and write with her in Majorca. Graves wrote that every poet needed a muse and, after his second marriage to Beryl Hodge he continued – perhaps to her exasperation – to fixate on other inspiring women. He also produced an influential collection of Greek myths, and historical fiction including *I, Claudius*.

Thomas Hardy (1840–1928) The Ruined Maid

Although Hardy is now best remembered for his classic novels including *Tess of the D'Urbervilles* and *Far From the Madding Crowd*, poetry was his first love and greatest ambition. His first wife Emma encouraged him in his writing, but the marriage was often unhappy. After her death, however, he found the memory of her to be a more inspiring muse than she had proved when alive. His second wife Florence patiently accompanied him on pilgrimages to places he and Emma had known and loved, where he could recapture the sense of that early love – and the guilt for his failings as a husband – and write about it.

Seamus Heaney (1939–2013) Blackberry Picking

Heaney's first volume of poems, *Death of a Naturalist*, was published in 1966. His work has examined the cycles of nature – you can often almost smell the peat – and the history and cultural identity of Ireland, inspired by his childhood in County Derry, Northern Ireland. He was awarded the Nobel Prize in Literature in 1995 and his acclaimed translation of *Beowulf* (1999) overcame competition from *Harry Potter and the Prisoner of Azkaban* to win the Whitbread Book of the Year Prize. Fans of his readings have, rather wonderfully, been called 'Heaney-boppers'.

George Herbert (1593–1633) The Elixir

Herbert was from a well-connected Welsh family: his glamorous mother, whose second husband was two decades her junior, was a patron of **John Donne**. After a brief academic and political career, he settled down happily to life as a country parson, and was much loved by his parishioners. All Herbert's poems have religious themes and many were later set to music as hymns. Puritanism was wrestling with the old Church traditions, but Herbert died of consumption before the Civil War would have forced him to pick a side. He left his poems to his friend Nicholas Ferrar with instructions to burn them or publish, as he saw fit, and Ferrar published. Charles I apparently took comfort in his collection, *The Temple*, before ascending the scaffold, so the verses must be very comforting indeed.

Thomas Hood (1799–1845) I Remember, I Remember / No!

Hood was the son of a London bookseller, and thought his hometown 'the world's greatest city', though he was hardly unbiased. He was initially best known as a comic writer. By all accounts he was also something of a wag in his personal life, though perhaps his humour has dated: he instructed his wife not to buy spotted plaice because it was rotten as a practical joke, when in fact all plaice have spots. His poem 'The Song of the Shirt' was a rallying cry bemoaning the terrible conditions under which the textile workers laboured, and it was a huge international hit.

Gerald Manley Hopkins (1844–89) Binsey Poplars / The Windhover

Hopkins's verse has a modern music that might explain why he never found an appreciative reading public amongst his Victorian contemporaries: his poems were not published until almost three decades after his death. This, along with his repressed homosexuality and his conversion to Catholicism (which rather horrified his family), might explain his gloominess. He became a Jesuit and, because he was rather tormented by how much he enjoyed writing, burned his early, Keats-flavoured poetry, vowing only to compose when his Church masters encouraged him to.

Horace (Quintus Horatius Flaccus, 65 BC–8 BC) O Fons Bandusiae / Happy the Man

Quintus Horatius Flaccus was the son of an aspirational freed slave, who educated him impeccably and enabled him to pursue a literary career during the reign of the Roman Emperor Augustus. Horace's odes often celebrate the simple life. He coined Latin phrases including *carpe diem* (seize the day) and *dulce et decorum est pro patria mori* (it is sweet and seemly to die for your fatherland: Wilfred Owen called this 'the old lie' in his blistering World War I poem of that title).

A. E. Housman (1859–1936) When I Was One and Twenty / Here Dead We Lie

Housman's most popular work was his self-published cycle of pastoral poems *A Shropshire Lad* – although he was actually born in Worcestershire and wrote the verses while living in London. He nurtured a passion for his fellow student at Oxford, Moses Jackson, but it was unrequited and he repressed his sexuality all his life. His nostalgic, melancholy verses struck a chord with readers hungry for an arcadian 'land of lost content', as he referred to Shropshire, especially during World War I. Among the phrases coined by Housman are 'blue remembered hills' – later used by Dennis Potter as a play title – and 'die another day', a slightly unlikely source for the name of the twentieth James Bond film.

Mary Howitt (1799-1888) The Spider and the Fly

Mary and her devoted husband William were prolific writers with over a hundred volumes to their names, including books on natural history and translations of Hans Christian Andersen's fairy tales. Though their fame has now waned, they counted writers including Dickens, **Wordsworth** and **Tennyson** among their friends, and even Queen Victoria was a fan. The dancing rhythm of this very Victorian moralizing verse inspired **Lewis Carroll**'s 'The Lobster Quadrille'.

Ted Hughes (1930–98) Hawk Roosting

A craggy Yorkshireman, Hughes spent his childhood hunting, shooting and fishing and lots of his rather macho poems celebrate the bloody, brutal elements of nature. His achievements have been overshadowed in the popular imagination by his tempestuous relationship with first wife **Sylvia Plath**, who killed herself after discovering his affair with Assia Wevill. Tragically, Assia later took her own life and that of their young daughter. Hughes became Laureate in 1984 and his final published work was the bestselling *Birthday Letters*, in which he at last addressed the fascinating relationship with Plath that saw him demonized for many years.

Leigh Hunt (1784–1859) Abou Ben Adhem

Hunt's journal, *The Examiner*, was required reading for the writers of the age, and he was close to most of them: **Shelley** was among the many who lent money to the jolly but profligate Hunt, Dickens based *Bleak House*'s Harold Skimpole on him and **Byron** apparently monopolized his children's rocking horse when visiting. He was a fearless journalist, even lampooning the decadent Prince Regent (later George IV). Calling him a fat 'Adonis' of fifty proved a barb too far, and Hunt was imprisoned, although he was allowed flowery wallpaper, a ceiling painted to look like the sky, books, visitors and even a piano in his cell.

Elizabeth Jennings (1926–2001) My Grandmother

Jennings worked briefly in publishing and as a librarian before becoming a full-time writer, living most of her life in Oxford. She once wrote: 'Only one thing must be cast out, and that is the vague,' a judgement reflected in her cool, concise style. Her Roman Catholicism and experience of mental breakdown in the 1960s both influenced her verses. Although she disliked publicly reading her poems, she became something of a mentor to student poets, whom she welcomed into her ornament-cluttered flat for discussion and tea. She was an avid consumer of cinema, and Häagen-Dazs ice cream.

Ben Jonson (1573–1637) On My First Sonne

On 'My First Sonne' catches Jonson in an unusually soft and reflective mood, as this moving verse is an elegy for his eldest son Benjamin who died at the age of seven. A successful and influential playwright – though his fame has been eclipsed by a certain contemporary, **Will Shakespeare** – Jonson was a man of contradictions. His elegant verses stand in contrast to his occasionally reckless behaviour: he was a drinker and a fighter, once killing a fellow actor with a rapier, although he managed to avoid being hanged for the crime.

John Keats (1795–1821) Ode to a Nightinglale / Endymion [extract]

Keats did not begin writing poetry until the age of eighteen, and he died young from tuberculosis – not, as **Byron** claimed, from the shock of being reviewed as a member of the 'Cockney School'. His output in such a short period is extraordinary. **Coleridge**, having greeted him, once said, 'There is death in that hand', and Keats himself predicted his own early demise. This only made him work harder, which did his constitution no favours. He offered his fiancée Fanny Brawne the option to call off their engagement as his health deteriorated, though she refused and remained unmarried for twelve years after his death. In later life, she told her children about her relationship with the Romantic poet but, understandably, had them swear not to tell their father.

Rudyard Kipling (1865–1936) The Way Through The Woods / The Glory of the Garden / If—

Kipling was born in Bombay and named after Rudyard Lake, where his parents had courted. Sent home from India to be schooled in England, he absorbed the Victorian ideals of duty and patriotism that colour much of his work, but writings including *Kim* and *The Jungle Book* link him for ever with India in the popular imagination. He had worked as a war correspondent and many of his best-loved poems deal with the wars of empire often – unusually for the time – from the common soldier's point of view. Kipling's 'If—' was voted the nation's favourite poem in a 1995 BBC survey and was inspired by the disastrous Jameson Raid that led to the Second Boer War.

Philip Larkin (1922-1985) An Arundel Tomb / MCMXIV

Larkin portrayed himself as the gloomy hermit of Hull, where he was the university's librarian for most of his career, though he did in fact have several love affairs with women including one of his assistants. His ambition was to write fiction, and he published two somewhat bleak novels, but it was his dry, plain-speaking poetry that proved popular, although his use of naughty words – especially in 'This Be The Verse' – caused controversy. Andrew Motion's 1993 biography uncovered some pretty unpalatable views Larkin held on race and women, but the popularity of his rather Eeyore-ish poems endures.

Larkin later admitted, in typically self-deprecating style, that in fact it was the right-hand gauntlet of Richard, Earl of Arundel that kept his hand free to clasp that of his wife, Eleanor, and not the left as 'An Arundel Tomb' claims. The effigies can be seen in Chichester Cathedral in Sussex.

Edward Lear (1812–1888) The Pobble Who Has No Toes / The Jumblies

Lear's 1846 A Book of Nonsense popularized the limerick form, but the man behind such jolly verses was brought up in poverty by his sister, and suffered from depression and epilepsy – a little understood and much feared condition at the time. Lear was an accomplished, albeit not very successful, artist and was even engaged to tutor Queen Victoria in drawing, although he never did quite get the hang of court etiquette. He travelled widely but always returned home to his much-loved cat Foss, who had lost his tail after an encounter with a snip-happy housemaid. Foss was evidently not so fond of travel: when Lear moved he had his new house designed as a replica of the old so as not to confuse his feline companion.

Lord Macaulay (Thomas Babington Macaulay) (1800–59) Horatius from Lays of Ancient Rome

Macaulay's father's was a prominent anti-slavery campaigner, and Thomas followed him into politics. In 1834 he took a position on the Supreme Council of India, where he had a vast impact upon the sub-continent's educational system, insisting on English being taught. Though talented, his attitude didn't always win him friends. Lord Melbourne said of him: 'I wish I was as cocksure of anything as Tom Macaulay is of everything.' Macaulay had a prodigious memory – he enjoyed challenges such as naming all the Archbishops of Canterbury backwards, so he must have been a riot – and he wrote many successful essays and histories. Only **Scott** and Dickens rivalled him in the bestseller lists of the day.

Notes on the Poets and Poems

Hugh MacDiarmid (1892–1978) A Drunk Man Looks at the Thistle [extract]

Hugh MacDiarmid began life as Christopher Murray Grieve, a postman's son. He was influenced by the experimental modernism of Joyce's *Ulysses*, and was ambitious and prolific in his writing. He published much in his own brand of Scots, which picked and chose from different dialects. A founder member of the National Party of Scotland, he was expelled for being a communist and joined the Communist Party, which duly expelled him for being a nationalist. MacDiarmid was a colourful character – 'I'll hae nae hauf-way hoose' was his philosophy – and he listed Anglophobia among his hobbies in *Who's Who*.

John Gillespie Magee (1922–41) High Flight

Born to missionaries in China, Magee was educated in England at Rugby School where he won the poetry prize that his idol, Rupert Brooke, had been awarded three decades earlier. His biography was, tragically, to mirror Brooke's in sadder respects, for he was killed, aged only nineteen, while training as a fighter pilot during World War II. This exuberant sonnet was inspired by a flight in a Spitfire, and is much loved by aviators and astronauts.

Katherine Mansfield (1888–1923) Camomile Tea

Born Kathleen Mansfield Beauchamp in Wellington, New Zealand, Katherine Mansfield is better known as a writer of short stories, including 'The Garden Party', than as a poet. A passionate and, by all accounts, occasionally difficult character, her love-life was bohemian and complicated: while pregnant with the child of another man, she married her rather older music teacher, only to abandon him days later. Rushed away to Bavaria by her mother, she suffered a stillbirth. Her second husband was writer John Middleton Murry, a somewhat helpless character with whom she enjoyed a rather more affectionate relationship through letters than in person. The constant presence of Ida Baker – the woman she called her 'wife' – was no doubt a bone of contention. The Murrys were close friends with the Bloomsbury set including D. H. Lawrence and his wife Frieda, with whom they lived for a time, though their relationship ended sourly. Lawrence sent Mansfield a vicious postcard calling her a 'loathsome reptile', and based the character of Gudrun in *Women in Love* on her. Her health was poor, and she eventually died of tuberculosis aged only thirty-four.

A. A. Milne (1882–1956) The King's Breakfast

Alan Alexander Milne will always be best known as the creator of honey-guzzling Winnie-the-Pooh. His collection of children's poems *When We Were Very Young* (1924) was an instant hit, as were other volumes including *Now We Are Six* and *The House at Pooh Corner*. The characters were modelled on his son Christopher Robin's stuffed animals, though in fact the now iconic images of Pooh were based by the illustrator on his own son's bear, Growler. Ashdown Forest provided the inspiration for many of Pooh's haunts; however, Milne's Sussex home, Cotchford Farm, attracted more dubious fame later when Brian Jones of the Rolling Stones drowned there.

Thomas Moore (1779–1852) The Last Rose of Summer

Thomas Moore, often seen as Ireland's bard in the way that Burns is Scotland's, was a famously charming man. So charming, in fact, that when Francis Jeffrey labelled his verses immoral and called him out for a duel, the two ended up chatting affably and became the best of friends. The son of a Dublin grocer, Moore became the toast of Regency society when his *Irish Melodies* and oriental verse romance *Lalla Rookh* were huge successes. He was a confidant of **Byron** and became his literary executor, though he burnt Byron's rather spicy memoirs at the behest of the poet's family. Among his other works were biographies of Sheridan and Byron (he did, after all, have inside information), and an unsuccessful history of Ireland.

Arthur O'Shaughnessy (1844–81) Ode

Born in London to Irish parents, O'Shaughnessy's day job was in the British Museum's Library, working in Icthyology (the study of fish). There was gossip that the bestselling writer Edward Bulwer-Lytton had pulled strings to get him the position there, and it had been suggested that he was Lytton's illegitimate son, though it is now believed that O'Shaughnessy's aunt, rather than his mother, was Lytton's lover. He was great friends with the artists of the Pre-Raphaelite Brotherhood and married Eleanor Marston, whose father was an artist and sister a poet. Their union was ill-fated: they had two children together, both of whom died young. Eleanor died only six years after their marriage, and Arthur followed her two years later.

Wilfred Owen (1893–1918) Strange Meeting

Owen enlisted to fight in World War I in 1915 but was sent to Craiglockhart hospital near Edinburgh in 1917 to recuperate from what was probably shell shock. There he met the established poet Siegfried Sassoon, and they bonded over their desire to write verses communicating the grisly reality of trench warfare to what they saw as a complacent reading public at home. At the time, Owen's truths were unwelcome: the patriotic dreaminess of Rupert Brooke's poetry was more to contemporary taste, for obvious reasons, but in subsequent years Owen has come to be hailed as the authentic voice of World War I poetry. He was never able to enjoy his popularity, however, as he was killed a week before the Armistice.

'Banjo' (Andrew Barton) Paterson (1864–1941) Waltzing Matilda

His home turf of rural New South Wales, Australia, inspired 'Banjo' Paterson, who borrowed his pseudonym from one of his much-loved horses. He was at various times a farmer, soldier, lawyer, novelist and journalist, though it is as a bush poet he is most celebrated. During his time as a war correspondent he covered the Second Boer War for the *Sydney Morning Herald* and also hoped to cover the Boxer Rebellion in 1901, although when he arrived in China he found that the conflict was already over. Paterson's collection of poems, *The Man From Snowy River*, was a publisher's dream, selling out its first print run in a week and racing through four editions in six months. He appears on the Australian $10 note.

'Waltzing Matilda' is Australia's unofficial national anthem: a 'matilda' is a travelling bag. The version here is from Paterson's original, rather than one of the many song versions.

Sylvia Plath (1932–63) Morning Song

Plath was fiercely ambitious and worked tirelessly on her poetry: her first collection, *Colossus* (1960), had been entitled, at various times, *The Bull of Bendylaw*, *Full Fathom Five*, *The Earthenware Head* and *The Devil of the Stairs*. She attempted suicide in 1953 and her subsequent experiences recovering in a clinic inspired her only novel, *The Bell Jar*. In 1956 she met **Ted Hughes** while studying at Cambridge University, and legend has it she bit his face. He was undeterred: they married and had two children, but the relationship broke down and, during the freezing February of 1963, she gassed herself, having first sealed the room to keep her children safe.

Edgar Allen Poe (1809–40) Annabel Lee

Poe's influence on literature is immense – his 'The Murders in the Rue Morgue' was one of the first detective stories – but in life he never achieved the success he felt he deserved. Orphaned at three, he spent an unhappy childhood with his warring foster parents; his military career ended with a dishonourable discharge; he failed his degree, was frequently in dire financial straits and drank heavily. No wonder his stories and poems have such a gothic gloom about them. He married his thirteen-year-old cousin Virginia, who died aged only twenty-four from tuberculosis. An early biographer of Poe, William F. Gill, obtained her bones when the graveyard was destroyed and used to display them to ghoulish dinner guests.

Alexander Pope (1688–1744) Ode on Solitude

It was just as well for Pope that he was able to carve out a decent living with his pen because, at that time, his family's Catholicism barred him from holding public office. He published essays and translations as well as verse, and eventually presided over a workshop operation similar to those of the great Renaissance painters, in which he added his inspired finishing touches to the fruits of his assistants' labours. Pope is best known for his delightfully vicious court satires – especially the mock-epic *The Rape of the Lock* – but also produced work, like this ode, in a quieter, pastoral style. His prosperity enabled him to settle in a fine house in Twickenham where he could potter about in his elaborately decorated grotto, the walls of which were encrusted with seashells.

Ezra Pound (1885–1972) Song in the Manner of Housman

Pound made quite an impression when he arrived in London from Pennsylvania: Ford Madox Ford describes his green trousers, pink shirt, single blue earring and sombrero. He was an attention-seeker, and once ate tulips in a pub to divert the limelight from **Yeats**. Pound's early work was rather flowery, but he was later involved in the Imagist and Vorticist movements, which produced sparer verse. He spent many years working on his extraordinary, many-layered *Cantos*, a vast undertaking that he never completed. He eventually moved to Italy, where he fell under the spell of Mussolini and adopted noxiously anti-Semitic views. He was brought back to America in 1944 but judged mentally unfit to stand trial for treason and was instead imprisoned until 1958, when he was released on the condition that he lived out his twilight years in Italy.

Henry Reed (1914–86) Naming of Parts

Reed achieved a first-class degree in Classics despite teaching himself Greek. He embarked on a freelance writing and broadcasting career during the boozy golden age of the BBC where his colleagues included Louis MacNeice and **Dylan Thomas**. Reed only published one volume of poetry. It contained 'Chard Whitlow', a parody of 'Burnt Norton' so accurate that even **Eliot** himself had to admit it was spot on.

During World War II Reed served in the Royal Army Ordnance Corps and at Bletchley Park, where the code cracking was done. He was an excellent impressionist and entertained his fellow troops by lampooning the weapons-training instructor. This comic turn found its final expression in 'Naming of Parts'.

Christina Rossetti (1830–94) Uphill / Remember Me

The devout and self-denying Christina was extremely unlike her rambunctious older brother Dante Gabriel Rossetti, a poet, party animal and founder member of the Pre-Raphaelite Brotherhood. She lived a pious life and, unusually for the age, never married, despite attracting suitors including the artist James Collinson. Remaining a spinster allowed Christina ample time to devote to poetry and good causes, including teaching and reaching out to fallen women, an occupation which also absorbed her brother from time to time, though in Christina's case it was carried out with a somewhat purer motive.

Sir Walter Scott (1771–1832) The Rover

Scott was inspired by the folk tales and history of the Scottish Borders, especially the Jacobite Rebellion some decades before his birth. He was the father of historical fiction, anonymously publishing several wildly successful blockbuster novels including *Ivanhoe*. These enchanted an international audience, despite Scott claiming later that he turned to prose simply because **Byron** 'beat' him at poetry. Speculation about the 'Wizard of the North' who produced the novels was rife, and Scott came clean in 1827. His long poem *Marmion* includes the celebrated lines 'Oh! what a tangled web we weave / When first we practise to deceive!'

Alan Seeger (1888–1916) I Have a Rendezvous with Death

After graduating from Harvard, where **T. S. Eliot** was a classmate, Seeger lived a bohemian lifestyle in New York's Greenwich Village. He developed a courtly and old-fashioned style and demonstrated a preoccupation with premature and glorious death that reflects sadly on his fate.

Seeger joined the French Foreign Legion in order to serve in World War I, the USA being neutral until 1917, and wrote this, his best-known poem, while convalescing in a field hospital after having bronchitis. He was killed in action in 1916 at the Battle of the Somme, and was reported to have died cheering on his fellow soldiers despite being riddled with machine-gun bullets. His poems were published a year after his death, and this one became a favourite of John F. Kennedy.

William Shakespeare (1564–1616) Sonnet 73 / Sonnet 130

Shakespeare's biography is shrouded in mystery, despite his incalculable influence on the canon of English literature and the very fabric of the language. His genius for moving and entertaining the frequently rowdy Elizabethan theatre audiences elevated him from humble beginnings in Stratford-upon-Avon to become a prosperous playwright. His 154 sonnets, published posthumously, were long neglected, though they have subsequently puzzled commentators: they are dedicated to a mysterious 'Mr W. H.' who may or may not be the same 'Fair Youth' to whom many of them are addressed. The later sonnets, including Sonnet 130, address a 'Dark Lady', whose identity – if she is not fictitious – has confounded critics. Suggestions have included Mary Fitton, one of Elizabeth I's ladies-in-waiting, the patroness Emilia Lanier or the racier Lucy Morgan, who graduated from being another of Elizabeth's maids to running a brothel.

Percy Bysshe Shelley (1792–1822) Ode to the West Wind / The Masque of Anarchy

Shelley was always a rebel, and his behaviour as a youth – including espousing atheism and eloping with the sixteen-year-old Harriet Westbrook – scandalized his aristocratic father. The idealistic young poet hoped that Harriet might raise their daughter in what he saw as the natural manner of animals – which would have involved a very long period of breastfeeding and a lot of naked running about – but Harriet sensibly refused.

Shelley later deserted poor Harriet, who drowned herself two years later while pregnant by an unknown man, to run off with, then marry, Mary Wollstonecraft Godwin. When they competed to tell the scariest fireside tale, Mary took the prize by composing the classic novel *Frankenstein*. Shelley perished in a boating accident in Italy, where the couple had settled, and his friends burnt his body on a pyre. They returned the charred heart to England and interred the ashes in Rome's Protestant Cemetery, which would probably have offended Shelley's anti-religious sentiments. Apparently, **Byron** pleaded to keep his adored friend's skull but his request was denied. As Byron was known to have had goblets made from the skulls of medieval monks, it was no doubt a prudent refusal.

Robert Southey (1774–1843) The Battle of Blenheim

Southey had planned to found a radical artistic community with the young **Coleridge**, sagely pointing out that they should probably study farming first, though the scheme came to nothing. This youthful revolutionary ended up as Poet Laureate and Charlotte Brontë wrote to him for advice: he praised her work, but kindly advised that women shouldn't really consider literary careers. **Byron** suspected Southey of having spread scurrilous rumours about him – rather unfairly, since the truth was generally quite scandalous enough – and mocked him throughout his poem *Don Juan*. Southey spent his latter years in a house in the Lake District stuffed with the remnants of other poets' families, including Coleridge's abandoned wife and children.

Edmund Spenser (*c.* 1552–99) *The Faerie Queen* [extract]

Spenser mingled with the poster boys of the Elizabethan court including Walter Raleigh, Sir Philip Sidney and the Earl of Leicester, though he eventually died penniless. The Earl of Essex paid for his burial in Westminster Abbey, and literary London turned out to throw pens and poems into the coffin in mourning.

The Faerie Queen is a hymn to the Elizabethan establishment, especially its leading lady Elizabeth I ('Gloriana'). Spenser originally planned twelve books though only just over six survive (to the relief of students through the ages, no doubt). After chasing payment with a poetic grumble in which he coined the phrase 'without reason or a rhyme', Spenser eventually secured a royal pension, though Elizabeth's adviser Lord Burghley thought him overpaid: 'all this for a song!'

Algernon Charles Swinburne (1837–1909) The Garden of Proserpine [extract]

Swinburne was educated at Eton, where he developed a fascination for flagellation, and Oxford, where he befriended the Pre-Raphaelite artists. His racy poems scandalized society, and he gave the impression of a private life to match them: one of his parties involved spirits instead of wine, pornographic pictures of young men, and a monkey. **Wilde**, however, suggested the supposed depravity was all an attention-seeking sham. Swinburne's health was fragile, and hard living and heavy drinking didn't help. When he suffered a breakdown, his loyal friend Theodore Watts-Dunton took him in to dry out and supervised him through the surprisingly respectable remainder of his days.

In classical mythology, Proserpine, or Persephone, was the maiden condemned to spend half the year in the Underworld, plunging the earth into winter, because she had eaten six pomegranate seeds – a rather unsatisfying meal to risk breaking the rules for.

Alfred, Lord Tennyson (1809–92) The Lotos Eaters / Mariana

Savage reviews of his early poetry caused Tennyson to stop publishing
for nearly ten years, but he went on to become Poet Laureate for much of
the Victorian era, and was even created a baron. Both Victoria and Prince
Albert admired his poetry and the Queen was especially moved by *In
Memoriam A. H. H.* – Tennyson's elegy for his much-loved friend Arthur
Henry Hallam – after the Prince's death. His subjects ranged from the
topical – 'The Charge of The Light Brigade' was written in mere minutes
after reading *The Times*'s report on this Crimean War disaster over breakfast
– to the archaic and Arthurian. As Tennyson was so short-sighted, he often
composed in his head and sometimes neglected to write his verses down. It
was Hallam who transcribed 'The Lotos Eaters'.

Dylan Thomas (1914–53) Fern Hill

Thomas was a fascinating raconteur and a heroic boozer, and his readings
were as popular for their unpredictability as for their brilliance. He could
evidently be exasperating, though, and was apparently given to pinching
items from friends' houses to sell. Two thirds of his romantic, lyrical poetry
was written in his late teens but, though dissolute, he wasn't lazy: 'Fern Hill'
apparently went through more than three hundred drafts. Thomas worked
for the BBC when he wasn't in the pub with his colleagues, and his radio
play *Under Milk Wood* was acclaimed. He had a predictably tempestuous
relationship with his wild wife Caitlin, who was known in her youth for
performing knickerless cartwheels; he died unsurprisingly young.

Henry Vaughan (1622–95) They Are All Gone into the World of Light

A rural Welsh doctor – and, evidence suggests, not a terribly good one –
Vaughan had a religious epiphany after the twin disappointments of the
defeat of the Royalists by the Parliamentarians in the Civil War and the
death of his brother Thomas during an unwise alchemical experiment. He
was something of a mystic, fascinated by the occult and the supernatural
powers of nature. After his first wife died, he married her sister and
produced a second family, which led to legal wrangling and, one imagines, a
few tense family gatherings.

Derek Walcott (1930–2017) A Far Cry From Africa

Walcott was born in St Lucia. His poetry shows the influence of Western
verse – the Elizabethans, **Wordsworth**, **Tennyson**, and Robert Lowell –

coloured by the rhythms of the Caribbean, and it is this mixed heritage and identity that shapes his distinctive voice. Walcott originally trained as a painter, and he also wrote numerous plays. He was awarded the Nobel Prize in Literature in 1992.

Oscar Wilde (1854–1900) Her Voice

Wilde was a leading light of the Aesthetic Movement, which advocated 'art for art's sake' and prioritized beauty above the moralizing values of Victorian society. He was feted for his successful plays including *The Importance of Being Earnest*, until his scandalous homosexual relationship with Lord Alfred Douglas, known as 'Bosie', enraged the boy's father, the Marquess of Queensberry. Queensberry sent Wilde a poorly spelled card calling him a 'posing somdomite', and Wilde ill-advisedly sued for libel. The ensuing trial saw a hysterical press pore over Wilde's lifestyle – including his liaisons with rent boys – and, though his famous wit won the most laughs in court, he was convicted of gross indecency and sentenced to two years' hard labour. His reputation never recovered, and he died in Paris after some sad years of poverty and ill health. One of his last utterances was said to have been, 'My wallpaper and I are fighting a duel to the death. One of us has got to go'.

William Wordsworth (1770–1850) Tintern Abbey / The French Revolution *from The Prelude* / Ice-skating from *The Prelude*

Wordsworth achieved great fame and success during his lifetime, after starting out as quite the firebrand (apparently, he threw terrible tantrums as a child and once skewered a family portrait with a fencing sword!). His use of natural rhythms of speech and language rather appalled the critics but proved popular with the public and, like his Romantic peers, he valued individualism, personal freedom and the wonders of nature. He was deeply fond of walking – often composing poems on the hoof while out with his adored sister Dorothy – and, though he lived to a ripe old age, it was his rambling that eventually dispatched him when he fell victim to pleurisy after walking in wet weather.

Wordsworth's autobiographical *Prelude* was published by his widow after his death. By the time it reached the reading public, the advent of the railways and encroaching industrialism had changed the face of Britain entirely, and the world it described was already as distant as its author's childhood.

W. B. Yeats (1865–1939) Aedh Wishes for the Cloths of Heaven / When You Are Old

Arguably Ireland's greatest poet, William Butler Yeats was a leading figure in twentieth-century literature. He spent some of his childhood in London but returned to Ireland in 1880 to indulge his passion for Irish culture, literature and politics. His impact as a journalist, orator and poet on Irish culture was such that one Irish senator said of him: 'He invented a country, calling it Ireland.' This vision of Ireland may be seen in his earlier works, like 'Aedh Wishes for the Cloths of Heaven', which are full of 'Celtic twilight'. Yeats fell deeply in love with the beautiful Republican revolutionary Maud Gonne (to whom the sonnet 'When You Are Old' is addressed) and proposed to her incessantly and fruitlessly over the years. Once he'd given her up, he abandoned his 'embroideries/Out of old mythologies' and became more modernist in his poetry. In 1917 he married the much younger Georgie Hyde-Lees, a marriage that proved surprisingly successful, and in 1923 he was awarded the Nobel Prize in Literature. In spite of being what he called 'a sixty-year-old smiling public man', he maintained a lifelong interest in spiritualism; he and his wife used to experiment together in séances and automatic writing.

SELECT BIBLIOGRAPHY

A Poet's Guide to Britain, (BBC 1 May 2009) [TV broadcast]

Abrams, M. H. (ed.), *Norton Anthology of English Literature Volume 1* (WW Norton, 1993)

Abrams, M.H., et al. (eds), *Norton Anthology of English Literature Volume II, Sixth Edition* (WW Norton, 1993)

Ackroyd, Peter, *Albion: The Origins of the English Imagination* (Chatto & Windus, 2002)

Andronik, Catherine M., *Wildly Romantic: The English Romantic Poets: The Mad, The Bad and the Dangerous* (Henry Holt, 2007)

Creighton, T.R.N. (ed.), *Poems of Thomas Hardy, A New Selection* (Macmillan, 1974)

Donoghue, Denis, *Yeats* (Fontana, 1971)

Drabble, Margaret (ed.), *The Oxford Companion to English Literature* (Oxford University Press, 2000, revised 2006)

Graves, Robert, *Good-Bye to All That* (Jonathan Cape, 1929)

Gross, John (ed.), *The New Oxford Book of Literary Anecdotes* (Oxford University Press, 2006)

Gurr, Elizabeth, and de Piro, Celia, (eds), *Nineteenth and Twentieth Century Women Poets* (Oxford University Press, 1997)

Hall, Donald (ed.), *The Oxford Book of American Literary Anecdotes* (Oxford University Press, 1981)

Hamilton, Ian (ed.), *The Oxford Companion to Twentieth-Century Poetry in English* (Oxford University Press, 1994)

Holmes, Richard, *Blake's Songs of Innocence and Experience* (Tate Publishing, 1991)

Hughes, Ted (ed.), *Sylvia Plath: Collected Poems* (Faber and Faber, 1981)

King, Pamela M., 'Metaphysical Poets', *York Notes Advanced* (York Press, 2001)

McDonald, Trevor, *Favourite Poems* (Michael O'Mara, 1997)

Motion, Andrew 'Foreword', *Great poets of the 20th century: Philip Larkin* (Guardian Books, 2008)

Moyle, Franny, *Desperate Romantics: The Private Lives of the Pre-Raphaelites* (John Murray, 2009)

Sampson, Ana (ed.), *I Wandered Lonely as a Cloud: . . . and other poems you half-remember from school* (Michael O'Mara, 2009)

Schmidt, Michael, *Lives of the Poets* (Weidenfeld & Nicolson, 1998)

Southam, B.C., *A Student's Guide to the Selected Poems of T.S. Eliot* (Faber and Faber, 1968)

Taggart, Caroline, *I Used To Know That: stuff you forgot from school* (Michael O'Mara, 2008)

Walter, George (ed.), *The Penguin Book of First World War Poetry* (Penguin, 2006)

Wavell, A. P. (Field Marshal Earl Wavell), *Other Men's Flowers*, Memorial Edition (Cape, 1952)

Wilson, A.N., *The Victorians* (Hutchinson, 2002)

Websites:

Note: there are individual websites for many poets, which are easily found online using a search engine. Only more general websites are listed here.

www.1911encyclopedia.org

www.americanpoems.com

www.answers.com

www.contemporarywriters.com/authors

www.davidpbrown.co.uk/poetry

www.digital.library.upenn.edu

www.ies.sas.ac.uk

www.literaryculture.suite101.com/article.cfm/writers_homes_in_britain

www.luminarium.org

www.oracleireland.com

www.poemhunter.com

www.poetryarchive.org

www.poetryfoundation.org

www.poetryintranslation.com

www.poetrysociety.org.uk

www.poets.org

www.spartacus.schoolnet.co.uk

www.victorianweb.org

www.warpoets.org

www.wikipedia.org

ACKNOWLEDGEMENTS

I would like to thank everyone – friends, family, colleagues and readers of *I Wandered Lonely as a Cloud* – who offered their opinions on the poems that should be included in this book. Special thanks to Toby for his boundless knowledge on every subject and to Natalie for her painstaking checking of the poems. My wonderful parents have been hugely supportive, as ever, and know all sorts of interesting things, and my husband Mark has brought me many gratefully received cups of coffee. However, I will not be thanking my cats Daisy and Tinker, who believe that a computer or manuscript is something to be firmly discouraged in a comfortable lap.

The author and publishers are grateful to the following for permission to use material that is in copyright:

Fleur Adcock: Extract from 'The Soho Hospital for Women' from *Poems 1960–2000* (Bloodaxe Books), copyright © 2000 by Fleur Adcock, by permission of Bloodaxe Books Ltd.

Allan Ahlberg: 'Scissors' from *Please Mrs Butler: Verses* (Puffin), copyright © 1984 by Allan Ahlberg, by permission of Penguin Books Ltd, a division of Penguin Random House.

W. H. Auden: 'Tell Me the Truth About Love' copyright © 1940 by W. H. Auden. Reprinted by permission of Curtis Brown, Ltd. All rights reserved.

W.H. Auden: 'Musée des Beaux Arts' copyright © 1939 by W. H. Auden. Reprinted by permission of Curtis Brown, Ltd. All rights reserved.

Hilaire Belloc: 'Jim, Who Ran Away From His Nurse', from *Cautionary Verses* (© Hilaire Belloc 1907), by permission of PFD (www.pfd.co.uk) on behalf of the Estate of Hilaire Belloc.

Select Bibliography

Hugh MacDiarmid: Extract from *A Drunk Man Looks at the Thistle*, Part 6, copyright © 1926 by Hugh MacDiarmid / 2004 by the Estate of Hugh MacDiarmid, from *Selected Poetry*, ed. Alan Riach and Michael Grieve (Fyfield Books, 2004), by permission of Carcanet Press Ltd.

A. A. Milne: 'The King's Breakfast' from *When We Were Very Young* by A. A. Milne. Text copyright © The Trustees of the Pooh Properties 1924. Reprinted by permission of HarperCollins Publishers Ltd © (1925) (A.A. Milne).

Sylvia Plath: 'Morning Song', from *Collected Poems*, ed. Ted Hughes (Faber and Faber), copyright © 1961, 1962, 1963, 1965 by Ted Hughes, copyright renewed, by permission of Faber and Faber Ltd.

Ezra Pound: 'Song in the Manner of Housman', from *Personæ* (Faber and Faber), by permission of Faber and Faber Ltd.

Henry Reed: 'Naming of Parts', from *Collected Poems*, ed. Jon Stallworthy (Carcanet, 2007), by permission of the Carcanet Press Ltd.

Dylan Thomas: 'Under Fern Hill', from *Collected Poems* (Phoenix), copyright © 1952 by The Dylan Thomas Trust, by permission of David Higham Associates Ltd.

Derek Walcott: 'A Far Cry From Africa', from *Collected Poems 1948–84* (Faber and Faber), by permission of Faber and Faber Ltd.

INDEX OF POETS

Index of Poets

INDEX OF TITLES, FIRST LINES
AND WELL-KNOWN LINES

Titles of poems are in **bold** type, first lines are in roman type, and familiar or well-known lines are in *italic* type following a headword in ***bold italics***.